ROCKWELL LECTURES
Rice University

JULIAN N. HARTT

The lost image of man

Louisiana
State
University
Press

To the memory of my father

ALBERT HARTT

who insisted upon *Henry Esmond*
but also upon Hawthorne, Poe,
Eliot, and Dickens as the staples
of the library of a prairie
parsonage, to say nothing of
Shakespeare and the Bible.

Preface

Since in the course of this essay I have offered nothing by way of justification—or even of excuse—for these timorous forays into the grand preserves of literature, such a word may not be unseemly here.

The theological indiscretions of literary people, artists, and critics, are not, altogether or any particular instance, a very good reason for this sort of counterattack. So let it suffice to say this: in my experience novels provide indispensable light upon the human scene, as well as high pleasure, and this is true of some minor works as well as of the acknowledged masterpieces. I do not suppose that my theological craft, such as it is, has given me an unique purchase either upon great or minor novels. But on the other hand the employment of such craft cannot be altogether beside the point in an age when people of wide variety are searching literature, among other things, for some kind of religious value; and seem often as disturbed by what they find thereof as when they find none at all.

This is not to say that I have made a point of seeking out the fiction in which the religious question is consciously posed or at any rate can be seized and delivered with symbolistic forceps, for I have not. The religious question—whatever that is—can in fact be avoided in our time with some grace. Of the human question this is not so. The novel at its best makes this surpassingly clear. Novels of inferior range and power make it clear enough.

It will be clear from the outset that I have refrained from judgments upon form, style, etc. On such matters I have opinions to spare, but they are not expert; and I have therefore ridden with but one opinion throughout concerning the novel itself: what a novelist says about the human condition in his novel can be discussed as a disclosure of a human reality, and as such altogether, that is as reality disclosed and as a form of disclosure, it is compact of moral conviction. We may wish to argue about the convictions—are they sound or unsound? But first we must see what he sees. We may not like it, but reality has a way of persisting despite our revulsions; and an authentic artist is for this purpose among the best of human tutors, so good, actually, that he is sometimes suspected of being in league either with divinity or with devils. I have not tried to settle the question.

New Haven, Connecticut
July, 1963

Acknowledgments

I wish to thank the following publishers for permission to quote passages from the works cited: Random House, Inc., for the quotations from William Faulkner's *Absalom, Absalom! Light In August, Go Down, Moses,* and *The Mansion;* and from James Joyce's, *Ulysses.* Charles Scribner's Sons, for the quotations from Ernest Hemingway's *Farewell to Arms;* and from Alan Paton's *Cry, the Beloved Country.* E. P. Dutton & Co., Inc., for the quotations from *Justine* and *Clea* by Lawrence Durrell. The MacMillan Company, for the quotations from Arthur Koestler's *Darkness at Noon.* The Bobbs-Merrill Company, Inc., for the quotations from *Lie Down In Darkness* by William Styron. Alfred A. Knopf, Inc., for the quotations from *The Plague* and *The Fall* by Albert Camus. The Viking Press, for the quotations from *In Dubious Battle* by John Steinbeck. Grove Press, for the quotations from D. H. Lawrence's *Lady Chatterley's Lover.* Farrar, Straus & Co., Inc., for the quotations from Alberto Moravia's *The Empty Canvas.*

The substance of chapters three, four, and five was presented as the Rockwell Lectures at William Marsh Rice University in May, 1962. I am pleased to have this opportunity to express my thanks to Dr. Carey Croneis for the invitation to do the Rockwell Lectures and to Professor Niels Nielsen, Jr., of the Rice faculty for valuable suggestions concerning the lectures.

Much of chapter two was presented as a paper to a meeting of the Society of Fellows of the National Council on Religion in Higher Education, in August, 1961. Mrs. Sallie TeSelle has put me in her debt by a close reading of that paper.

I wish also to thank Mrs. Tenney Leas for her skill in creating an excellent typescript from my long-hand and for additional editorial work. Mrs. Dorothy Clair has given me invaluable editorial help, and I wish to record here my thanks.

Contents

The lost image of man

The crisis of the image

The mood in which I sing is not lamentation, and the purpose is not another flagellation of that woeful creature, Modern Man. We are quite accustomed to hearing this creature abused for his many grievous sins, and we all take a turn at prophesying the final terrible end of the human enterprise.

Perhaps we deserve to hear the worst about ourselves, but in this essay I have a more modest ambition: to suggest certain ways in which our culture has cancelled its heritage, for better or worse. Some will say that those elements of the cultural heritage had lost their meaning anyway. Others will hold out hope for a miraculous renewal of the great past in some age to come before (or as a substitute for) the death of the human race. Assuredly each of us has a right to judge such conclusions for himself. But before we move to judgment, whether generous or merciless, ought we not probe our understanding of our situation? I think we ought to do so; and this essay is presented in that connection.

II

For this purpose we shall be dealing with *images* rather than with abstract conceptualizations. This is but one way of announcing that art, rather than science or philosophy, is the human realm through which we shall try to track the spirit's struggle with destiny, death, damnation, and resurrection.

Perhaps I ought to offer a theory to justify this choice of "realms," a theory about the immersion of the human mind in reality not its own and not itself and about the unique account of such reality the artist, child and master of imagination that he is, provides. I do not offer such theories here. I have, to be sure, made a trial run at some theoretical questions, particularly touching upon the achievement of the artist and the response we make to it. The authentic response to the artist's achievement is a movement of imagination in which we grasp the reality of his evocation and disclosure. Whether we agree with him is beside the point if by agreement we mean assenting to a propositional proposal. The artist may believe that human life is a bad joke in an insane universe, but his art (unless he is a charlatan) will not be a mere didactic, homiletical exercise devised to make that point. Where didacticism is art it captures and distills the flavor of realities other than doctrinal propositions, and this requires non-conceptual instruments. The prime instrument is the "image," and it may be a word, a gesture, a mass, a line, a sound. In this image the beholder himself sees, feels, *is,* the reality expressed. The reality in which the artist offers participation is condensed in an image and is not otherwise available. Therefore we do not look to the artist either for a plain circumstantial account of the world or for a logically coherent theory about its meaning. From the artist we may learn what it is to be immersed in such and such reality—immersed, caught up in it, possessed by it, awareness of it sharpened and strengthened immeasurably and unbelievably beyond conventional expectations.

III

The phrase "conventional expectations" is important for this essay, first because it directs attention to a sad and perhaps fateful confusion: the virtual identity of Heritage and Convention in the popular mind. Artists may be as afflicted by this confusion as the rest of us, but for our own good we would hope not. Whether or not an artist does his first work in the style of an acknowledged master (which in fact is generally the case), he knows that he lives in a tradition which gives structure to his own venture. He may limit himself to the resources of that tradition. He may reject it, or reduce its onetime magisterial authority by his own inventions. His rebellion and reductions may express loyalty to the *real* tradition and a revulsion against its corruptions. This may be, and it may not; which is to say that the artist may also confuse Heritage with Convention.

What then do we understand by "Convention"? A convention is a commonplace treatment of a reality; it is a reality disguised in widely accepted appearances. For example to say that monogamous marriage is a convention in our culture calls attention both to widely pervasive normative attitudes toward sexuality *and* to frequent deviations in practice from those norms. Accordingly the conventional, in morals as in art, is the object of deeply ambiguous loyalty. It is impossible to have a human world without conventions. It is also impossible to have a living world so long as the conventions of the old one are unchallenged. So we are impelled on the one hand to pay ungrudging respect to the everyday decencies—the normalities of perception, judgment, and conduct—and, on the other, to insist that human richness cannot be wrought from the everyday decencies alone.

The perennial tension between creativity and convention has been greatly heightened by the crises wracking the world. The newspaper every morning chants crises political and economic.

We cannot count upon the press to disclose the quieter (and quite possibly the more desperate) crises and disasters. Yet we know without the help of the mass media that now we cling to the conventions for dear life, and in the next moment try to find the whole of meaning in the repudiation of the conventions. *This panic flight to and from the conventional life is a capital expression of a deep crisis in the image of man.* We are having great difficulty in getting a clear, steady, and amiable image of ourselves. Lacking this center of reference for understanding and evaluation, we are strongly inclined to accept whatever dogma and image is doing a brisk business in the market, even if they are incompatible either with the good conscience of conventionality or the demands of creativity.

IV

To make what we ought of the distinction between Heritage and Convention, we must explore the image itself. "Image" is commonly used to signify a representation of something in the mind, for example, the image of a tree is a perception. Commonsensically we suppose that the tree itself is represented in this perception but has its own being outside the mind, and so the tree-image is treated as a more or less authentic "copy" of the real tree. "More or less faithful" because the mind and the tree are (presumptively) different beings. The mind infuses and environs the image with feelings peculiar to its own (psychic) life, and we easily suppose that the tree itself does not infuse its own being with such feelings.

From here image goes in two directions. Symbolic life is one. Ontological mimicry is the other. At first glance these two goals appear irreconcilable to each other.

The movement of image to symbolic life is the impetus given to the crystallization of perceptual form by emotion. Thus the Cross, tree symbolized, achieves a remarkable independence from the visual entity. The symbol is *expressive*. The visual entity by itself is placed in a "field" without reference to any feeling-tone. In the symbol a perceptual form (or quality) persists and is part (and perhaps the foundation) of the concreteness of the symbolic image; but as symbol the image no longer refers to a field in which entities are externally related to one another.

Image also goes in the direction of "ontological mimicry" or "duplication." This goal is hinted at in the statement, "the son is the very image of the father"; or, in a famous philosophical figure, "Time is the moving image of Eternity." Such usages —and no more so the latter than the former—suggest a philosophical principle: some things have being in two (or more) "places" simultaneously, one of which is prior to the other, both in respect to temporality and power. The father must be first and in some sense foremost. In another sense some property apparent in the father first and then in the son, itself has the duplicative power and is therefore before either the son or the father and determines the being of both.

The immemorial model of ontological duplication is the artist's imagination in relation to his production or performance. Here the prior and prime reality is supposed to be an idea in the artist's mind; and the production is the copy, always in some respect or another imperfect, if in none other than in the sheer fact of being a copy and thereby existing "outside" the mind.

This famous model is itself made possible by a remarkable assumption: *the perfect artist* (a being therefore in some sense divine) has a genuinely originative imagination, i.e., one that does not depend upon any external being for its material or "inspiration." Whether the perfect artist is therefore the first cause of every other being is a famous theological dispute.

Ontological duplication and the symbolic image do not run so swiftly and so far from each other as we might have first supposed. In fact we begin to anticipate and perhaps even predict their convergence. The symbolic image is the product of imagination; and imagination by virtue of its power is an ontological first principle. Thus the poet is either a "god" himself or one who participates in the properly divine life of—creation!

In our world we do not quite know what to make of the notion of the master, "divine" imagination and so we are tempted to dismiss it as myth. But who is the superlative genius who created such a myth?

When we do try to make something of the master imagination, one of two ambitious ideas may easily seem coercive, if not cogent. (1) The ontological first principle is an "absolute mind"; (2) the *real* creators of the human world are the poets.

As to (1) we are now prone to understand this as a vast sea of unconsciousness from whose depths the eternal symbols arise into clarity of expression. Where this metaphysical-psychical imagery falls short of plausibility, one can put hand to "collective minds" short of the absolute at least in power, if not in coherence: "public opinion," the "mind of the Negro," the tribal spirit, etc., are so many appeals to a master imagination greater than the individual person and yet not lord of the cosmos.

The "collective unconscious" in its sociological, psychological, and historical reduction is not clearly an improvement upon the Absolute, as the agonizing over cultural relativism demonstrates. So the (2) option comes into its own, i.e., that the poets are the real creators of human history.

This (2) becomes more likely when we ask more closely after the reality of human history. No more than music is actually in the printed (or memorized) score, is history actually in documents and artifacts. The primary "place" of history, its mode of being, is the imagination. There the deed which occurs in the public world is truly consummated, i.e., endowed and infused with value. So the public acts are but the potentialities, the possibilities, of history. They are acts perhaps only dimly inspired and loosely governed by reason and seem therefore to be but random occurrences, but they become history only when they bow the neck to the dominion of imagination.

Thus the first and greatest historians of a people are its epic singers. They forge the consciousness of the race and are therefore the masters of all artificers. But this of course is to make symbols of Homer and Dante, of Milton and Shakespeare. In fact the master poets would be powerless were there no poet in each man brooding over the dark depths to speak and hear the creative word. "Imagination" is the name of *that* poet. What that poet does goes far beyond receiving what is spoken by another spirit—although it is the inner ear, with a vengeance. This poet is also genuinely and profoundly originative: by the imagination the past and the future are connected to form a meaningful whole apprehended in and as the present moment. If that connection is not strongly and clearly established, life is corrupted either by nostalgia (the disease of memory) or by longing (the disease of expectation). If the connection is wrong, the shape of the present moment may be either too threatening or too trivial to be endured.

The shape of the present moment is also the image the person projects of himself. It is only in such a form that the person is really present to himself. Unclarity of that form is the same as unrealized human potentiality or as that dimness of being of which the ethical dimension is irresoluteness.

The situation in which the person has his being is also comprehended in the shape of the present moment. "Situation" is at once structure and powers. *The existentially decisive reality both of structures and powers is representational.* Nonetheless they may speak to the person in and of their own authority, quite as though they, rather than the person, governed their representation in his mind. Why should they not? That the "mind is able to become all that it knows" testifies as certainly to the power of the knowable world as to the suppleness of the mind.

Both as symbol and as ontological first principle the image is a singular unity of possibility and actuality. The master imagination, for instance, must be in perfect command of its powers and thus is an actual agent. But it commands something *in its own being* not yet actualized; and the more masterly its competence the more clearly and fully immanent in its own being is this potentiality.

The symbol is also a study in the concrete polarity of actuality and potentiality. It has formal actuality or it is nothing; and it has this so perfectly that men speak of its "eternality." But it is also replete with potentiality: the *essential* being of a symbol is its representational power, and this power is *always* latent in part. The symbol can never be discursively exhausted (a principle sometimes confusedly expressed as the "non-translatability of the symbol"), but this means that its essential being is its power to evoke, convey, and direct the passions, as an immanent cause thereof. Thus viewed as an historical datum a symbol has a kind of eternal reality; whereas, as an immanent cause of passion it is always emerging from latency with a thrust calculated and ordained to carry it to dominion over the passions. This thrust may miscarry, so disastrously that the passions thereafter thrash about to no point except sheer statement, and life falls away into that flawed image of power and peace we rightly see in the alternation of violence and apathy.

In this essay I have tried to trace the fate of spirit in our world as a history bound into the fate of master images.

V

The exercises in theory now behind us we can settle with dispatch what we have acknowledged as the confusion of Heritage and Convention. The Heritage is, fundamentally, the master images in which Western man has grasped his being—what he is and ought to become. Heritage also is the continuity of the modes in which these images have been expressed—the "media" as well as the "styles."

"Convention" is the reduction of a mode of expression to stereotype and cliché. From this follows—with what dreadful rapidity and finality we can all sense—the trivialization of the images themselves. Thus "passion" is converted into sentimentality, and "image" is converted into a target for psychological manipulation.

In this confusion "tradition" is a word invoked to arrest rather than direct change, and "creativity" is used to invoke rather than redeem revolution. A more worthy way than either exists, or so we must believe. The problem is to find it.

VI

In this essay I have delineated but few aspects of the crisis of the human image. For this purpose I have not made a point of consulting only those artists who have bad news for ourselves and our world, in order to let some one else sport the mantle of true and terror-inspiring prophecy. On the other hand I have not lingered long with writers animated by a desire to "speak comfortably to Jerusalem." One is grateful to those who believe sincerely "that it is better to light a candle than to curse the darkness." But can one really be instructed by those who insist that there is no night, while we all stumble blindly and grope for something to lean upon? Although it was uttered long ago, the curse laid against false prophecy is still binding: "Woe to them who cry 'Peace! Peace!' when there is no peace."

The death of the epic image

The wealth of epic traditions in Western culture is so great that to speak of *the* epic image seems to strike a doubtful note at the outset. One thinks of Homeric epics, the biblical epics, Virgil, Dante, and Milton; and of the mighty achievements of Melville and Conrad, and of Faulkner. This is not even a fair hint of the wealth. Ought one therefore begin by supposing that each epic tradition must have its own distinctive representation of Man in the World, since an epic celebrates the heroes of a people, and we are overwhelmed by the variety of history? The question serves to quicken an argument: where the epic image (whatever it is) fails, the people as an historic community is threatened with extinction. So many today confess a strong presentiment of the collapse of the epic image. They feel that this age does not have the raw material suitable for the imaginative creation of great heroes: the drama and the novel are peopled by moral pygmies, emotionally regressive adults, and intellectual flyweights; altogether they seem as far beyond the plain man's courage as their philosophies are beyond his understanding—and interest, too, for that matter.

It is hard not to read these feelings as omens of doom for the Western heritage. One may so read as one runs. Here a more prosaic task confronts us, namely to characterize what we began by calling the epic image.

(1) Epic art has an aspect I call religious: it relates events and expresses the appropriate emotions of man's engagement with cosmic powers. These powers are not necessarily estimable in human eyes nor is the issue of encounter with them necessarily desirable or fortunate; but man has no choice except to deal with them as best he can.

(2) Man is peculiarly exposed, uncovered, delivered, to the action of the cosmic powers. Particular theological beliefs are, of course, very important in the determination of the particular spirit of an epic, and these beliefs vary across a broad spectrum; but it is astonishing how little these differences matter so far as the reality of "exposure" is concerned. The Homeric heroes, Socrates, Israel, the messianic saint of Second Isaiah, Jesus, Captain Ahab, Faust, Kurtz, Beckett—they are all, in all the variety of individual manner, peculiarly vulnerable to the invasion of power from beyond the human community. They are all marked men, and the marks are noted, if not made, by the gods.

The mode and the reason of "exposure" vary, as we should expect. Yet in this variation a constant appears: the epic hero is larger than life-size, although not necessarily better than common men. Something of essential human existence, and of the historical community, is in him realized in its purity—courage, strength, wisdom, fidelity, piety, patience. whatever it is, it is in the hero in a largeness and clarity of realization which elevates him, not above the human condition, but above the anonymity and facelessness of the crowd-mass of the community; above, that is, mankind still obscure, unrealized, unbirthed, in the matrix of biological and cultural necessity.

By virtue of his "largeness and clarity of realization" the epic hero is "exposed." He is exposed at once to the special attention of the gods and to the ignorance, cowardice, and treachery of the crowd-mass and its exploiters. He is engaged in a mighty conflict in which the future of the people is being determined, but he cannot depend upon the beneficiaries for comfort or aid.

(3) Nevertheless the hero is the representative of the undifferentiated and unrealized crowd-mass in his encounters with the great powers. He struggles for a good greater than his own life. The crowd, for its part (and quite understandably), has a habit of witnessing the struggle from a safe distance, taking no greater chances than curiosity, vindictiveness, or an unclear premonition of the immensity of the stakes, requires. Thus the epic hero is what any man would have to be to stand up to the incredible invasion of the cosmic powers—would have to be but characteristically is not and has no real desire to be. The crowd-man is covered, hidden, secreted; or so fancies himself, and thanks the gods for these blessings; but eventually he also thanks them for the gifts of heroes.

Whence then the hero? What accounts for his courage, strength, piety, or what not by which he is elevated above the crowd and exposed to the dread powers, thereby making it possible for the community itself to be elevated and enlarged in the power of its life? The formative epics of Western culture do not attempt to answer in our categories, moods, and modalities of explanation. The gift or achievement of heroic life, as well as the celebration of its greatness and efficacy, may well be an essential element of the epic itself. The hero *may* be of divine origin or under divine inspiration and comfort. He may be son of Heaven and darling of its resident powers. To our modern minds this is but a way of expressing the "mystery of leadership," or, more specifically still, the baffling phenomenon of authority in human affairs. The epic itself is not concerned with making great capital of these mysteries since its burden is the actual efficacy of the hero's presence in the community. Moreover, the essential medium of his power is his human substance rather than his putatively divine origin. Thunderous his footfall may be, and marvelously resourceful and valiant his spirit; but withal he is exemplar of the human being. He is a bodily presence; he is a man who has a place and a people. He is the son of a human community. He exists to defend that community against all evil and bring its good to richest flowering.

(4) A real human community is thus both the "presupposition" and the "objective reference" of the epic image. The epic is a creation of the community, which means that a unitive human state of affairs is assumed by an epic and the values and spirit of that community are celebrated rather than created by its epics. What is thus achieved may come to be held as a model of moral instruction for generations thereafter, but the meaning of the epic is not in the first instance performatory or prescriptional. Certainly from the expression of the people's real history the hearer is bound to conclude to the desirability of some enlargement and purification of his own existence, but the first object of the epic is the adequate representation of the true history. The community is thus the "objective reference" of the epic: it is that for which the epic is told. It is designed to evoke the emotions appropriate to the reception of the true past.[1] This must not lead us to suppose that the real past is over and done with. Here its epic art unmistakably serves to remind the community that its time is an unbroken continuum and that the proper reception of its real past is a preparation for the future, if the epic heroes have indeed grappled with the divine cosmic powers.

The dark epics of Melville and Conrad do not appear at first glance to efface or dim the essential reference to a community. Ahab, for instance, is a man swept into damnation and death by an obsessive hatred of evil—a theme quite sufficiently dark for any taste except sheer morbidity. Yet he is committed to the destruction of this evil; or, if it be but illusion, he will somehow get behind it to the awful truth, to reality terrible in its blankness and emptiness. Although he does indeed have a place, a homeland, and a people, the cosmic dimension of his conflict suggests a matching universality of benefit derived from it: not simply an old bitter score settled in a private duel between Moby Dick and Ahab, but the sea delivered from its abominable scourge. Ahab is not, he is decidedly not, a neurotic man who seeks only to expel an evil dream from his outraged psyche in order to enjoy happiness, or—a more likely end in view for our own age—to enjoy untrammeled sleep.

At second glance a profound uneasiness about these late epic creators sets in. The epic hero always drinks deeply of the cup of solitariness; but Melville's heroes, and Conrad's, seem no longer representative men in the sense suggested under (3). They seem not to be the first of a new species dug by enormous expenditure of flesh and spirit from the primordial matrix, but, rather, solitary figures who pit themselves, in ultimate gestures of defiance, against overpowering evil—the blackness of the world. Men may be profoundly affected by their efforts, as Marlow is by Kurtz in Conrad's *Heart of Darkness;* but the community is not by so much, or by so much alone, given new life. *But perhaps the community does not exist for them and in them.* Perhaps for Melville, and for Conrad too, the community which alone creates the epic and can be instructed by it has vanished.

Perhaps the sheer *factuality of society,* in all its fortuitousness, had already begun to submerge the *validities of community.* If so, the fifth characteristic of the epic image is barely left visible.

(5) This final characteristic might properly be viewed as a recapitulation of the others. The epic relates the making or breaking of a community; it deals with men whose actions determine history and whose appearance in a community is therefore epoch-making for it. So great are the stakes, momen-

tous the occasion, and immense the powers arrayed against each other, in the epic vision.

II

If the epic now seems quite beyond the attainment and perhaps even beyond the understanding of the contemporary world, it may be profitable to ask how such a crippling blow was delivered? It was delivered as a "factualistic" resolution (or settlement, at least) of tensions of imagination, and thereafter of conscience, generated by the idealistic outlook and made unbearable by historical developments.[2] We have to say "factualistic" rather than "empirical" if we want to express properly the attitudinal depth involved: the nearly obsessive preoccupation with the reality-value of psychic immediacies ("facts") of both internal and external reference. It is almost as though sensitive and discerning spirits had experienced the shipwreck of all aspirations geared to anything whatever beyond these immediacies and had fled for comfort to a metaphysics (rather than a religion) which gave ready assurance that nothing else really exists, an assurance clearly beyond the competence of a rigorously empirical mind. As Frederic Henry says in *Farewell to Arms:*

I was always embarrassed by the words sacred, glorious, sacrifice. . . . We had heard them, sometimes standing in the rain almost out of earshot, so that only the shouted words came through, and had read them, on proclamations that were slapped up by billposters over other proclamations, now for a long time, and I had seen nothing sacred, and the things that were glorious had no glory and the sacrifices were like the stockyards at Chicago if nothing was done with the meat except to bury it. There were many words that you could not stand to hear and finally only the names of places had dignity. Certain numbers were the same way and certain dates and these with the names of places were all you could say and have them mean anything. Abstract words such as glory, honor, courage, or hallow were obscene beside the concrete names of villages, the number of regiments and the dates.[3]

Thus often and terribly men in the modern world have been betrayed by *ideals* into grotesque denials of the flesh's reality and weakness and into the most vapid sentimentalities. Mankind, Peace, Justice, Country, God—what ideal has *not* proved both corruptible and corrupting?

III

James Joyce's *Ulysses* is the capital illustration of the recoil from the epic vision into "factualistic" certitudes. One of its most remarkable features is a high and rich lyricism now (and once and for all, we are tempted to add) disengaged from the epic sense for any purpose other than the sheerly rhetorical, that is, the use of the devices of persuasion to reinforce a point, an attitude, a proposition, achieved independently of the work of art. Joyce develops with marvelous rhetorical cunning the passions appropriate to a view of things whose truth is taken for granted. Where the epic traditions had been profoundly metaphysical in instinct, as distinguished from dialectical sophistication, *Ulysses,* as a unitive achievement, comes to rest in factualistic tranquillity. Thus it behooves us to consider the way in which *Ulysses* jettisons the epic image item for item.

(1) and (2) The sense and shape of engagement with the cosmic power is gone altogether. To be sure broken elements of a once normative sacramental order of life are not lacking. Indeed such elements play an important role in the procession of the novel, but their role is no longer that of purveyors of an organic truth. This situation greets us in the opening scene: the organic unity of the Eucharist is already shattered and odd fragments are used for comic effect.

Stately, plump Buck Mulligan came from the stairhead bearing a bowl of lather on which a mirror and a razor lay crossed. A yellow dressinggown, ungirdled, was sustained gently behind him by the mild morning air. He held the bowl aloft and intoned: *Introibo ad attare Dei.* Halted, he peered down the dark winding stairs and called up coarsely: —Come up, Kinch, Come up, you fearful jesuit. Solemnly he came forward and mounted the gunrest. He faced about and blessed gravely thrice the tower, the surrounding country and the awaking mountains. Then, catching sight of Stephen Dedalus, he bent towards him and made rapid crosses in the air, gurgling in his throat and shaking his head.[4]

I do not at all want to suggest that Joyce's interest here is to blaspheme, or to call in question philosophically the traditional religion, or to propose an alternative faith.[5] *Ulysses* is not even deeply committed to the mild iconoclasm of anticlericalism. The battle is over, and it only remains to announce the results with brilliant rhetorical flourishes. This is what Joyce has done. He does it by showing us the structure and life of Stephen Dedalus' psyche, Dedalus the "fearful jesuit," the "jejune jesuit." Buck Mulligan, of course, *is* blasphemous.

—The blessings of God on you, Buck Mulligan cried, jumping up from his chair. Sit down. Pour out the tea there. The sugar is in the bag. Here, I can't go fumbling at the damned eggs. He hacked through the fry on the dish and slapped it out on three plates, saying: *In nomine Patris et Filii et Spiritus Sancti.*[6]

But Dedalus has a tortured conscience and Mulligan does not. Stephen remembers in agony his mother's death.

Her glazing eyes, staring out of death, to shake and bend my soul. On me alone. The ghostcandle to light her agony. Ghostly light on the tortured face. Her hoarse breath rattling in horror, while all prayed on their knees. Her eyes on me to strike me down. *Liliata rutilantium te confessorum turma circumdet: iubilantium te virginum chorus excipiat.* Ghoul! Chewer of corpses! No, mother. Let me be and let me live.[7]

Confronted by the vision of his mother, when he is in the

brothel—it is the fantastic Night-town sequence—he again cries out:

The corpsechewer! Raw head and bloody bones![8]

Which is followed by the anguished:

Shite![9]

Then, in a strictness of psychic, rather than logical, consequence:

Non serviam![10]

To his mother's last plea:

(in the agony of her deathrattle) Have mercy on Stephen, Lord, for my sake! Inexpressible was my anguish when expiring with love, grief and agony on Mount Calvary.[11]

Stephen replies:

Nothung![12]

Hereupon the nightmare is shattered, momentarily, by Stephen's lashing out with his cane and breaking a chandelier.

Thus Stephen agonizes mightily. The antagonist is memory. The conflict is intrapsychic.

The proud potent titles clanged over Stephen's memory the triumph of their brazen bells: et unam sanctam catholicam et apostolicam ecclesiam: the slow growth and change of rite and dogma like his own rare thoughts, a chemistry of stars. Symbol of the apostles in the mass for pope Marcellus, the voices blended, singing alone loud in affirmation: and behind their chant the vigilant angel of the church militant disarmed and menaced her heresiarchs. A horde of heresies fleeing with mitres awry: Photius and the brood of mockers of whom Mulligan was one, and Arius, warring his life long upon the consubstantial-

ity of the Son with the Father, and Valentine, spurning Christ's
terrene body, and the subtle African heresiarch Sabellius who
held that the Father was Himself his own Son. Words Mulligan
had spoken a moment ago in mockery to the stranger. Idle
mockery. The void awaits surely all them that weave the wind:
a menace, a disarming and a worsting from those embattled
angels of the church. Michael's host. who defend her ever in
the hour of her conflict with their lances and their shields.[13]

Here Stephen Hero muses on the epic struggles of the Church
against the creators and fomentors of heresy. What he does
not do is to order his reflections to some "decision," either
affirmative or negative, concerning the faith of the Church. He
does not really believe that Mulligan is in any real danger from
Michael's furious angelic host. Obviously, Stephen is not
stranger to the words of ancient faith. The words simply do
not "add up," they are fragments of a world shattered forever.
The hero is timid, irresolute, unmanned.

Leopold Bloom is even further removed from epic encounter
and conflict. Preoccupied with death throughout the day,
although not centered or focussed by it, he is unable to find,
or to lament his failure to find, anything in it but mere grim
final fact:

Mr. Kernan said with solemnity:
—*I am the resurrection and the life.* That touches a man's inmost
heart.
—It does, Mr. Bloom said.
Your heart perhaps but what price the fellow in the six feet
by two with his toes in the daisies? No touching that. Seat of
the affections. Broken heart. A pump after all, pumping thou-
sands of gallons of blood every day. One fine day it gets bunged
up and there you are. Lots of them lying around here: lungs,
hearts, livers. Old rusty pumps: damn the thing else. The resurrection and the life. Once you are dead you are dead. That
last day idea. Knocking them all up out of their graves. Come
forth, Lazarus! And he came fifth and lost the job. Get up!
Last day! Then every fellow mousing around for his liver and

his lights and the rest of his traps. Find damn all of himself
that morning. Pennyweight of powder in a skull. Twelve grammes
one pennyweight. Troy measure.[14]

And what shall we say of Molly Bloom, the Great Mother
figure? Assuredly she herself has no "encounters" and is not
afflicted with any "instinct for the Transcendent." She is something of a "divinity" in her own right but a thoroughly natural
one, and in nothing suggesting a form or a power larger than
life. She is the eternal feminine but without the slightest trace
of romantic mystery, to say nothing of the supernatural. So
it is better to say that she is the everlasting female of the species,
sexually, not "spiritually," alluring, indestructibly fecund
although with but two issue of her body, and one dead at that,
to show for it. Primordially generative, source of life's heat,
fulfiller of desire, creature of desire; and thus and therefore the
one alone to whom the "Yes," if not the "Amen," can be en-
trusted.

> . . . and yes I said yes I will Yes.

But before we leap upon this famous concluding sentence of
Ulysses for metaphysical enlargement, we ought to remember
that her Yea-saying is part of the remembrance of her first
sexual union with Bloom; and that it is said by a luxuriantly
sexual woman who has not made a vice out of saying "No" to
mankind generally; and that she may just possibly be deciding
to do the thing which launched her soliloquy in the first place:

> Yes because he never did a thing like that before as ask to get
> his breakfast in bed with a couple of eggs.[15]

So there is no claimant for the epic stature and role, no
protagonist of mysterious origin, formidable in authority and
power, resolute past faltering, valorous beyond imagination.
Actually such a one appearing would be an anachronism, a wild
disfigurement of the world of *Ulysses*. The heroes are dead;

and the last aspirant, Parnell, had obvious flaws; and anyway he failed. Stephen, whose soaring dream of heroic achievement is hymned in such graceful irony in *Portrait of the Artist as a Young Man,* dreams no more in that vein, unless drunk: he has become the fearful jesuit, a scapegrace unlicensed theologian, a poet who does not write poetry, a man named absurdly after an ancient Greek mythological figure.

The failure here must be understood as essential to the human condition rather than as a sad declension from the grandeur of an authentically heroic age. This is made abundantly clear in the wonderful—and endless—scene in the saloon after Dignam's funeral. Here again the modality is comic; not the bizarre comedy of Night-town; but the daylit comedy in which the putative greatness of Ireland's, and mankind's, past is hilariously dissolved in and by laughter.

> —By Jesus, says he, I'll brain that bloody jewman for using the holy name. By Jesus, I'll crucify him so I will. Give me that biscuitbox there.
> —Stop! Stop! says Joe.[16]

So Bloom unceremoniously departs, dog snarling at his heels, biscuit box sailing past his ears. But Joyce gives it the full inflated treatment:

> A large and appreciative gathering of friends and acquaintances from the metropolis and greater Dublin assembled in their thousands to bid farewell to [Hungarian names of] Bloom. . . . The ceremony which went off with great eclat was characterized by the most affecting cordiality. An illuminated scroll of ancient Irish vellum, the work of Irish artists, was presented to the distinguished phenomenologist on behalf of a large section of the community and was accompanied by the gift of a silver casket, tastefully executed in the style of ancient Celtic ornament. . . .[17]

A mighty conflict, this! and a moving conclusion:

> And the last we saw was the bloody car rounding the corner

and old sheepface on it gesticulating and the bloody mongrel
after it with his legs back for all he was bloody well worth to
tear him limb from limb. Hundred to five! Jesus, he took the
value of it out of him, I promise you.[18]

But there is an epic version, also:

When, lo, there came about them all a great brightness and
they beheld the chariot wherein He stood ascend to heaven. And
they beheld Him in the chariot, clothed upon in the glory of
the brightness, having raiment as of the sun, fair as the moon
and terrible that for awe they durst not look upon him. And
there came a voice out of heaven, calling: Elijah! Elijah! And
he answered with a main cry: Abba! Adonai! And they beheld
Him, even Him, ben Bloom Elijah, amid clouds of angels ascend
to the glory of the brightness at an angle of forty-five degrees
over Donohoe's in Little Green Street like a shot off a shovel.[19]

Throughout the whole section the cunningly and outrageous-
ly inflated rhetoric does the trick intended: the greatness from
which we who now walk the earth are got, is illusion, a creature
molded in windy overreaching language.

(3) What then has become of the ultimately serious, the
future-binding issues in which the epic heroes contended? They
too are the stuff of saloon talk, to be treated either in the flat
discourse of everyday human commerce or in the lyric life of
the inner mind which suffers not the domination of factuality
except as grist for the powers of fancy.

Ineluctable modality of the visible: at least that if no more,
thought through my eyes. Signatures of all things I am here to
read, seaspawn and seawrack, the nearing tide, that rusty boot.
Snotgreen, bluesilver, rust: coloured signs. Limits of the diaphane.
But he adds: in bodies.[20]

Everywhere the momentous is threatened with extinction at
the hands of the commonplace buttressed by odds and ends
of scientific knowledge. Accordingly the common realities,
stripped of all sacramental meaning—all power, that is, to hint

in their weakness, and in their strength to give body to, immensities of Good and Being beyond the visibilities—become repugnant, vile, disorienting:

> His heart astir he pushed in the door of the Burton restaurant.
> Stink gripped his trembling breath: pungent meatjuice, slops of
> green. See the animals feed.
> Men, men, men.
> Perched on high stools by the bar, hats shoved back, at the
> tables calling for more bread no charge, swilling, wolfing gopfuls
> of sloppy food, their eyes bulging, wiping wetted moustaches. A
> pallid suetfaced young man polished his tumbler knife fork and
> spoon with his napkin. New set of microbes. A man with an
> infant's sauce-stained napkin tucked round him shovelled gurgling
> soup down his gullet. A man spitting back on his plate: half-
> masticated gristle: no teeth to chewchewchewit. Chump chop
> from the grill. Bolting to get it over, Sad booser's eyes. Bitten
> off more than he can chew. Am I like that? See ourselves as
> others see us. Hungry man is an angry man. Working tooth
> and jaw. Don't! O! A bone! That last pagan king of Ireland
> Cormac in the schoolpoem choked himself at Sletty south of
> the Boyne. Wonder what he was eating. Something galoptious.
> Saint Patrick converted him to Christianity. Couldn't swallow
> it all however. . . .
> . . . .
> Every fellow for his own, tooth and nail, Gulp, Grub. Gulp
> Gobstuff.
> He came out into the clearer air and turned back towards
> Grafton street. Eat or be eaten. Kill! Kill![21]

This is perhaps sufficient warning against concluding that nothing serious occurs in the psychic world. After all people are born—a promisingly serious start, at least one from which we do not recover until we die; and die we do and somedays we cannot think of anything else; and the full range of human vicissitude runs between the first arrival and the last departure. But this course has relation to no significant more-than-human order of things. By itself this does not entail (or express) the loss of humanistic passion; but when this loss of felt contact with a more than human order is coupled with a radically naturalistic, say rather *factualistic* account of human existence, the result does spread ruin across the humanistic enterprise. Men learn greatness—if they learn it at all—from great encounters. But if by real nature they have (or so believe) no capacity for greatness in any case and there are no great powers to be dealt with, the very idea of the same must be committed (ashes to ashes dust to dust) to the lyric of subjectivity and given voice either in the wistful or the comic mood.

> The whirr of flapping leathern bands and hums of dynamoes from the powerhouse urged Stephen to be on. Beingless beings. Stop! Throb always without you and the throb always within. Your heart you sing of, I between them. Between two roaring worlds where they swirl, I. Shatter them, one and both. But stun myself too in the blow. Shatter me you who can. Bawd and butcher, were the words. I say! Not yet awhile. A look around.[22]

The scene ends when Stephen encounters his younger sister, Dilly, as he rummages among secondhand books. He learns from her (he is not living at home) that some of his own books have been pawned. As he gazes at her the inner poet says:

> She is drowning. Agenbite. Save her. Agenbite. All against us. She will drown me with her, eyes and hair. Lank coils of seaweed hair around me, my heart and my soul. Salt green death.
> We.
> Agenbite of Inwit. Inwit's agenbite.
> Misery! Misery![23]

What more affecting expression of the human condition could we ask, given the disappearance of any sense of life and order beyond consciousness?

(4) The epic sings the greatness of a real community and the gifts of life, goodness, and glory made to it by its heroes. Here *Ulysses* has aspects that jar on each other as well as cancel the epic image.

We cannot mistake that *Ulysses* acknowledges a people, the

Irish; or that the greatness of this people lives only in memory; or that the memory is raddled with illusion of grandiosity. There is of course the element of another community in Leopold Bloom, the Jewish, but Bloom is beyond the reach of that community. A wanderer he, a sojourner in an alien land, but not one of a company. Even less than his Irish associates does he own a tradition which he holds in filial reverence and for the glory of which he is ready and equipped for doughty enterprise.

Community, in other words, has become a factual entity. It is constituted of the givens of blood, language, and fortuitous association. It is therefore itself a creature of *fate* rather than of destiny.

(5) *Ulysses,* accordingly, has no traffic in epoch-making events. The day, the dramatic interval, is "a day like any other day." Unless one watches for it fairly closely the calendar day slips past unnoticed: June 16, 1904. History, at least history in the sense of the destiny of a community, is not made on that day. True, notice is taken of a great disaster reported in the morning press:

[Mr. Kernan speaks] . . . I'll take just a thimbleful of your best gin, Mr. Crimmins. A small gin, sir. Yes, sir. Terrible affair that General Slocum explosion. Terrible, terrible. A thousand casualties. And heart-rending scenes. Men trampling down women and children. Most brutal thing. What do they say was the cause? Spontaneous combustion: most scandalous revelation. Not a single lifeboat would float and the firehose all burst. What I can't understand is how the inspectors ever allowed a boat like that. . . . Now you are talking straight Mr. Crimmins. You know why? Palmoil. Is that a fact? Without a doubt. Well now, look at that. And America they say is the land of the free. I thought we were bad here.

I smiled at him. *America,* I said quietly, just like that. *What is it? The sweepings of every country including our own. Isn't that true?* That's a fact.

Graft, my dear sir. Well, of course. where there's money going there's always someone to pick it up.

Saw him looking at my frockcoat. Dress does it. Nothing like a dressy appearance. Bowls them over.[24]

Thus the historic event is submerged in saloon cliches—in what today we should call "everydayness." Consequentiality is smothered by the psychic and social givens. The emotional response (reaction) to events and persons is the definitive response, and the emotional takes its cue and achieves its warrant from the inner stress of the psyche ("agenbite of inwit"). What then is at hand, or within the range of the imagination, to give rational or moral structure to that inner life? To what good beyond the exigent psyche is a person answerable? From what conflicts may he expect to gain wisdom? What failures will instruct him and what achievements ennoble him? What will glorify the community and the race of Man? What ought to be avoided as an evil thing worse than death?

In the world of *Ulysses* such questions have an outlandish air; but this is not because lesser men now walk uncertainly where once a breed of giants made thunder echo from their stride. Rather, the world as a creation of imagination has lost the epic dimension. Now men know that wish is father of the thought and every dream of glory is child of disordered appetite. So Bloom-Ulysses is master of fact, after a fashion; and wholly slave of fancy:

In what posture?
Listener: reclined semilaterally, left hand under head, right leg extended in a straight line and resting on left leg, flexed, in the attitude of Gea-Tellus, fulfilled, recumbent, big with seed. Narrator: reclined laterally, left, with right and left legs flexed, the indexfinger and thumb of the right hand resting on the bridge of the nose, in the attitude depicted on a snapshot photograph made by Percy Apjohn, the children weary, the manchild in the womb.
Womb? Weary?
He rests. He has traveled.
With?
Sinbad the Sailor and Tinbad the Tailor and Jinbad the Jailer and Whinbad the Whaler and Ninbad the Nailer. . . .
When?

Going to dark bed there was a square round Sinbad the Sailor roc's auk's egg in the night of the bed of all the auks of the rocs of Darkinbad the Brightdayler.

Where?[25]

Shades, shards, and random detritus of all the epics, legends, myths, and dreams, holy and profane, of wandering Man on this earth! All order shattered past all remembering, and all love: the elements thereof come weirdly together in a litany of Fact!

So at the end as in the beginning the lyric mood is conjoined with the factual, but the marriage is dubious, smacking strongly of fraud. The lyric sings the destiny of psyche in the factual world: a creature of passion it marks the unreality of passion's world. In the end the odds overwhelmingly favor the triumph of Mulliganism over Dedalus and Molly over Bloom.

Yes: Bloom-Ulysses comes home. Outward bound he fell amongst trials and temptations and wandered helplessly in the land of death, but from nothing is he delivered by valor or cunning, to say nothing of the powers of guardian deities. And at the end, irresistibly lured by the Great Mother thinly disguised as Penelope-Molly, he is safely home, one among many suitors to have occupied Molly's bed and Molly herself in his life's wandering.

IV

What image of man appears typically in *Ulysses* as the replacement of the epic image? Typically: Stephen Dedalus and Leopold Bloom, since, with the exception of the experiment with which the book concludes, the movement and shape of the world are gathered in from their perspectives. So: Man is the dream-haunted, dream-harried wanderer in an unintelligible bourne stretching from birth to death. His actual life is within the causal nexus; but this web of Ananke is not a consequential order in which a thread may be followed from ignorance to knowledge, folly to wisdom, darkness to light. The world image is not a mountainous wilderness debouching at last and miraculously upon a fertile sun-drenched plain peopled with the children of light; or the dense forest in which a clearing opens; but the labyrinth in which every route circles upon itself, involution upon involution, with no end except cessation of effort and no center except the heart's desire. Linearity in life's pursuit thus cancelled, on what can the mind feed except itself? And how shall the spirit know whereof it exists save by the sound of its own voice? But the sounds, the words, do not march to the beat of drums beyond the psyche: they come and go, rise and fall, to the stress and yield of the psyche determined out of all reason from the murky depths. Perhaps this explains the astonishing master-image of Man in *Ulysses:* the talker, the word-spouter, the sound-artificer, the fabulous artificer— of words.

Homo rationis has been gone so long we can hardly remember his appearance. And now *homo agens* has joined him in limbo: he is but a memory-image conjured *ex nihilo* by *homo vocis,* or perhaps now just *Vox.* "In the beginning was the Word"; and the word was: Talk.

V

Let us be clear as to our intention: we are not set up in business as judge or jury of the artist's performance in *Ulysses.* If he has done what he set out to do our quarrel must be with the world, not with him. He has created the model anti-epic for our time, the model because he so cunningly employs features and elements of the epic traditions of Western history to expose the full reality of the epic's death in the modern world. He renders in a concrete metaphor the world modern man has created out of his imagination. He does not actually retell the ancient epic of Ulysses, he uses it as a framework externally related to the consciousness of his characters—and to ours. For we too inhabit a world alienated from the epic vision. Altogether? No; but the epic possibilities have been reduced remarkably, in number and dignity, to the point where we can run over them quickly:

(1) Warfare
(2) Anticonventional existence
(3) Reflections of the Christ-epic
(4) The Communist Revolution

(1) War in the twentieth century is at least a stage grand enough for the epic imagination. Here the whole of mankind must extend itself in terrible effort to remain alive. A vaster conflict we dare not imagine, nor one giving greater scope to courage, patience, and wisdom. Yet how many epic heroes have actually arisen out of these world-shattering events? Why have more claimants for these honors come from the First World War than from the Second World War? Perhaps we can settle for the second question, to which the answer surely seems to be: in the First World War men still believed that *patris,* and perhaps even *humanitas,* was worth dying for. They commonly accepted a mysterious providential consummation of their minute efforts, effected somehow and somewhere beyond the outrageous face of circumstance. So the obscurity of the heroes (the fact that they fell far below the requisite dimensions and qualities of the classical tragic figures) has, if anything, a direct rather than inverse relation to their achievement, since it is the sublime self-overlooking quality of their actions, and thus their availability to the inscrutable providential ordering, rather than their personal natures, that matters. The hero is no longer the exposed man, he is the obscure man trapped by great events. And even though simple to the point of witlessness, he is able to summon courage, self-respect, and the will to die for the Cause.

The Second World War found Western society in a very different "spiritual" situation. Even though the cause seemed much clearer, that is, the dreadful reach of the ambitions of cruel men was much more obvious, fire-power was technologically developed to the point where courage counted for very little, comparatively. But an even more important theological alteration had occurred: men had a drastically diminished confidence in Providence; and the vision of a life-giving and inclusive community had become very dim; and men had little motivation and less raw material for representing themselves as the stuff of heroes. Thus men are depressed not merely by what now seems the sure knowledge of their littleness and total vulnerability before immense social forces, but also, and more decisively, by a growing conviction, growing both in strength and plausibility, that those forces are not governed by reason either human or divine. In this situation the epic has no intelligibility. Brave and humane people have not disappeared from the novel and the drama. If *Ulysses* is right, the stories of their mortal years simply cannot be told as epic, except, of course, ironically.

Yet, and it is odd enough, man in the condition of war makes possible *For Whom The Bells Tolls,* a novel more nearly epic, in serious vein, than any other in our time. Pointless as the military objective around which the novel moves may be to all involved in it, or nearly all, some at least have a sense of a larger meaning in which, by courage—and chance!—they may participate.

The Korean War shows how much farther (and in what a short time!) our world has receded from the epic possibility. Here the forbidding face of *pointlessness* dominates the scene; and imagination recoils from it by snatching desperately at private and domestic values as though they could somehow be totalled to constitute a significant and coherent reason for living and for dying. The Nation is no longer *Patris,* the beloved Fatherland. Home is the cuddly (and probably unfaithful) wife, the convertible (car, that is), the well-paid job, the country club, the tranquil fireside, etc. In other words, Reason has departed from violent social conflict, perhaps forever, except for the Marxist theologians, about whose faith in historical Reason most of us feel we would do better to love our madness. But with the flight of Reason from conflict, indeed, from the substance of the common life, the epic possibility vanishes; and thus the kingdom of Man is diminished, impoverished, and placed under sentence of the final death: pointlessness.

(2) Anticonventional existence offers some promise of epic fulfillment in our culture, by which we mean a life committed to the achievement of a good (and perhaps a power) impossible under the constraints of "everydayness." Certainly here an antagonist of giant size and power is available: the massive institutional life of our culture with its correlative generalized attitudes of acquiescence, if not complicity, in its antipersonal dictates. So the "picaresque saint"[26] emerges in literature.

Amiable rascals in the novel have been with us for a long time. Perhaps in the hands of an ironist such characters are always to be understood as a rebuke to the trivialities and illusions of the standard life. But the burden of human meaning and good comes only very lately to rest upon the intransigent spirit, the man who does more than rail at conventionality; he takes arms against it and at least in his own person beats it to death in the interest of freedom. He is the Rebel; and whether he is cheerful or surly, insouciant or bitter, he knows the power of the enemy and hurls himself into the fray nonetheless.

With what sadness, therefore, do we come to realize the futility of the picaresque hero's struggle! self-confessed at that. By his own efforts he may save his own soul. In the words of Hugo in Sartre's *Dirty Hands,* he is "unsalvageable"; but the world is well lost for all of him. Far be it from him to be a maker or bearer of destiny for a historical community! He is not cast in the role of representative man, and he has not the slightest impulse or intention to identify himself with the fate of the crowd-man.

I think we can identify that component of the epic vision

decisively lacking in the anticonventional thrust: the belief in, the appeal to, any teleological principle real or valid over against the Rebel. Ignazio Silone's heroes are particularly interesting and affecting figures just here. For they are rebels *with* a cause and the cause is Humanity, the community of mankind. Yet they are beyond comfort of Providence: the Christian scheme is either archaic or the victim, together with the people, of ecclesiastical maladministration and malfeasance; and the Marxist scheme is also ruined either metaphysically or by the ruthless machinations of the power-mad Communist party. Hence the hero's love of the human community has no historical embodiment, and none is foreseeable, and none lies within the dominion of honest hope, except in their own solitary hearts and the evanescent, fragile face-to-face relationships open to them. Their heroism is real but it is all spirit and no "body." They are true nobility of a nonexistent ethical kingdom; their several stories are all antiepics, although not executed with Joyce's fearsome mastery, except insofar as they retell unconsciously in their own being some aspect or element of the Christ-epic, and notably that aspect of self-sacrifice in love for the blessing of the human community, or, even more ambitiously put, for the proper glory thereof.

The anticonventional hero may indeed have a sense of history; he may know that this is the last time around for even the elementary human values and perhaps even for human life. So he fights the good fight out to the end, necessarily alone, necessarily, not freely, not joyfully. He is uninstructed by Providence and is wholly devoid of any confidence in the arrival on the human scene, in his lifetime or ever thereafter, of the hosts of righteousness. Destiny is unseated and undone. History is in the deathless unbreakable grip of Fate.

(3) The Christ-epic is still with us. I do not mean a conscious design to create a Christ-symbol for our time but, rather, the expression of some element or aspect of that "sacred history" in characters not really imitative of the original hero of

the Christ-epic except in moral attribute. Our art forms are not yet through with the representation of the travail of innocence in this wretched unfeeling world; and the powerlessness of true goodness; and the misunderstanding of selfless love; and the reality of vicarious sacrifice, etc. Certainly each of these in this random incomplete enumeration offers some possibility of epic achievement. But each is a fragment, a disconnected and alienated quality attached mechanically to a substance indifferent if not hostile to its prosperity. In its brokenness the Christ-epic is without power to reveal a life and world ordered to the realization of good however violently abusive and arrogant the forces of evil may be for the moment.

So the fragments, the fugitive qualities, of the Christ-epic serve but to accent the predicament of spirit in the world and are not to be taken as being even impossibly cryptic hints of the ultimate order of human affairs in inclusive Being and Good.

We have again then to confess that testimony to courage, innocence, love in its outreach, downreach, upreach, patience, hope, wisdom, what not, fails of epic achievement, perhaps also of epic ambition, because the requisite and appropriate ontological presentments are lacking. The affairs of spirit which matter most are by common consent the ones, precisely, in which we are least likely to be engaged with the "really real" powers determining our lives and the future of the world.

(4) A perfectly obvious claimant for epic honors and glory is the revolutionary movement of the modern world: Communism. Certainly here we should expect to see great things, since a teleological order is presupposed, there are giant antagonists seeking each other out in deadly certitude, and the destiny of a real community is at stake.

Ah, yes: but what is actually presented? The heroic age, a great epoch now ended; and literature so heavily doctrinaire as to be dogmatic exercises; and bitter disenchantment with the false gods of Communist piety from those who have bowed the knee. I confess cheerfully that I find the last sort by all odds the most instructive, not merely, I hope, because it flatters antecedent ideological commitments I may be guilty of having made. Not for that reason, I hope, but because here at last the radical disparity, indeed the alienation, of personal determination from the absolute teleology, is acknowledged. The laws of history engulf and absorb personal determination; but not as the first or prime party of an analogy masters the second party, because the "person," the "I," is a grammatical fiction, a metaphysical error. The web of necessity is not spun by the will, it masters the will. Therefore passion is an effect and never a cause. Therefore love of the great cause, say of social justice, does not actually make any objective determinations. Appeal to such a passion may prove to be a rhetorical necessity but history is not made by rhetoric.

It is supposed by some that the Marxist theology is thus revealed as subject to the same deadly paradoxes which infest traditional Christianity. Does not the faith of our fathers also exhibit ultimate confidence in an order and power which override all human agency and give to the latter therefore only an illusion of efficacy? Is there not a striking similarity of rhetorical indulgence, the sinner summoned to repentance and amendment of life, the believer fired with zeal to change the world, etc.?

The similarities are deceptive and pursuit of them is finally pointless. The traditional faith of the church honored (or, if you prefer, posited) a positive relationship linking personal existence and the ultimate Being. This relationship was not limited to solicitude on the part of the Creator for every creature of his making, but it extended into an analogy of being. The whole world is an effect of will, the ultimate order of being is responsive to the necessities of the Good. *Man is the image of God and not simply a determination of His causality.*

It may be that the party takes on some of the characteristics of the epic image. Certainly it appears to be the real hero of Marxist fiction. The hero in any other sense would violate the canons of "Social Realism."

Here and there the people, rather than the party, is the hero in the epic struggle against the imperialistic enemy. But does the people produce representative men from whom history takes its cue? Or is the people the real individual?

This is not a merely rhetorical question. Even the doctrine of the party may contain a residue of a community which affirms rather than cancels genuine personal individuality. If it does not then the Marxist hero is no better off than the submerged middle-class citizen into whose fantasy-life, even, hardly the ghost of the epic image survives *(pace: The Secret Life of Walter Mitty!)*.

III

The dream of innocence shattered

An important aspect of the traditional image of man is suggested by the phrase "the corruption of innocence." In Western culture man has been represented as a creature whose primordial condition is unsullied and uncomplicated purity. This condition is ruined by his encounter with evil either too subtle for the comprehension of such a naif or too massive for his small powers.

In fine this is Adam's story. It has been rendered in rich variety, from which I single out a contemporary American version, that of William Faulkner. I do this because America has produced its own mythic image of Adam and in doing so illustrates, and perhaps encourages, a significant confusion; and Faulkner is a handsome case in point.

The American image is a man miraculously delivered from the corruptions of the Old World. He is a new being in a new land. He is Nature's (and probably God's) darling child, violent, generous, uncomplicated, resourceful, blindly egoistic; and in all his faults and virtues, irrepressibly loveable. In this image Innocence and Purity are one confused moral substance. Analytically we must try to distinguish them from each other as follows: Innocence is a vagueness of boundary between one's own being and other beings; Purity is freedom from guilt. The innocent person may in fact be properly chargeable with wrong-doing, but his self-awareness is so primitive that he suffers no guilt. The desire for purity presupposes awareness of self as guilty. Innocence once lost is irrecoverable—there is no return to Eden, except in fantasy. Purity is recoverable, not as the restoration of virginity but as the discovery of the right relation of one's purposes and drives to what is good in itself. It follows that the shattering of the dream of innocence is a more painful and ruinous episode than the loss of purity.

II

The "dream of innocence" is the representation of the world as congenial and perhaps actually pledged to the fulfillment of one's good if one but be true to one's own nature: because one matters more than anything else, to oneself.

In *Absalom, Absalom!* Faulkner has painted a great portrait of an innocent, Thomas Sutpen. It is a story of violence in which the innocent himself is destroyed, but not before he has made his name a curse.

When he was a poor white boy, years before the Civil War, Thomas Sutpen's pride was mortally injured by the aristocratic landed gentry of tidewater Virginia. In his innocence he recoiled from this unintentionally cruel blow, and in his innocence he launched his long and cunningly wrought career aimed at redress. In time he becomes one of the legendary founding fathers of Yoknapatawpha County, Mississippi, carving a large estate out of the wilderness, building an immense plantation mansion, finding a woman to occupy it, getting her with child, once, a boy, and twice, a girl. All of this pertains to his grand design, to which, in his innocence, everybody and everything is "adjunctive."

Sutpen's cunning, courage, and diligence are welded together to become a curse. He is himself haunted by a very live ghost from his past, his son by an earlier marriage to a woman with some Negro blood; and who, mother and child alike, he had simply and in clear conscience deserted because of the blood-taint he had finally discovered. In his innocence he had always taken what he wanted and discarded it when it no longer served his purpose. This habit of soul, this nature, leads to his own violent death and to heartbreak, dishonor, and suicide for others in generations to come. But to the end, when his world is coming unstitched at all the seams, he is genuinely puzzled over what went wrong with a life-scheme so clearly conceived and unrelentingly pursued:

> "You see, I had a design in my mind. Whether it was a good or a bad design is beside the point; the questions is, Where did I make the mistake in it, what did I do or misdo in it, whom or what injure by it to the extent which this would indicate. I had a design. To accomplish it I should require money, a house, a plantation, slaves, a family—incidentally, of course, a wife. I set out to acquire these, asking no favor of any man. I even risked my life at one time, as I told you, though as I also told you I did not undertake this risk purely and simply to gain a wife, though it did have that result. But that is beside the point also: suffice that I had the wife, accepted her in good faith, with no reservations about myself, and I expected as much from them. I did not even demand, mind, as one of my obscure origin might have been expected to do (or at least be condoned in the doing) out of ignorance of gentility in dealing with gentleborn people. I did not demand; I accepted them at their own valuation while insisting on my own part upon explaining fully about myself and my progenitors: yet they deliberately withheld from me the one fact which I have reason to know they were aware would have caused me to decline the entire matter, otherwise they would not have withheld it from me—a fact which I did not learn until after my son was born. . . ."[1]

Guilt, if he felt it at all for anything he did, was secondary to some failure of calculation or execution.

The instrument of this innocent's destruction is a creature of his own molding, Wash Jones. Wash has been Sutpen's lackey for many years, in war and peace, and sees him as a man of towering strength and unalterable purpose. In fact he has more or less cheerfully acquiesced in Sutpen's sexual use of his granddaughter—it is still part of Sutpen's grand design to have a son. When Wash's granddaughter is brought to bed with child, Sutpen comes to the cabin, learns that the baby is a girl, and rejects contemptuously the mother and his own "get." Not until then does the realization come to Wash that neither Wash nor Wash's family matter to Sutpen as much as his horses do.

> . . . he watched Sutpen emerge from the house, the riding whip in his hand, thinking quietly, like in a dream: *I kaint have heard what I know I heard. I just know I kaint* thinking *That was what got him up. It was that colt. It aint me or mine either. It wasn't even his own that got him out of bed* maybe feeling no earth, no stability, even yet, maybe not even hearing his own voice when Sutpen saw his face (the face of the man who in twenty years he had no more known to make any move save at command than he had the stallion which he rode) and stopped: "You said if she was a mare you could give her a decent stall in the stable," maybe not even hearing Sutpen when he said, sudden and sharp: "Stand back. Dont you touch me" only he must have heard that because he answered it: "I'm going to tech you, Kernel" and Sutpen said "Stand back, Wash" again before the old woman heard the whip. Only there were two blows with the whip; they found the two welts on Wash's face that night. Maybe the two blows even knocked him down; maybe it was while he was getting up that he put his hand on the scythe. . . ."[2]

Thus Sutpen, the innocent, is brutally destroyed by his servile human tool.

The second innocent is Joe Christmas of *Light in August*.
He is much more the victim than a builder of a fate. He knows
that he is a bastard. We learn eventually who his parents are.
He does *not* know whether he is Negro—and neither do we.
He sees his whole life as flight; he is always running down a
long road to a certain doom at the end.

He stepped from the dark porch, into the moonlight, and with
his bloody head and his empty stomach hot, savage, and cour-
ageous with whiskey, he entered the street which was to run for
fifteen years.

The whiskey died away in time and was renewed and died
again, but the street ran on. From that night the thousand streets
ran as one street, with imperceptible corners and changes of
scene, broken by intervals of begged and stolen rides, on trains
and trucks, and on country wagons with he at twenty and twenty-
five and thirty sitting on the seat with his still, hard face and
the clothes (even when soiled and worn) of a city man and the
driver of the wagon not knowing who or what the passenger
was and not daring to ask. The street ran into Oklahoma and
Missouri and as far south as Mexico and then back north to
Chicago and Detroit and then back south again and at last to
Mississippi. It was fifteen years long: it ran between the savage
and spurious board fronts of oil towns where, his inevitable serge
clothing and light shoes black with bottomless mud, he ate crude
food from tin dishes that cost him ten and fifteen dollars a meal
and paid for them with a roll of banknotes the size of a bullfrog
and stained too with the rich mud that seemed as bottomless as
the gold which it excreted. It ran through yellow wheat fields
waving beneath the fierce yellow days of labor and hard sleep
in haystacks beneath the cold mad moon of September, and the
brittle stars: he was in turn laborer, miner, prospector, gambling
tout; he enlisted in the army, served four months and deserted
and was never caught. And always, sooner or later, the street
ran through cities, through an identical and well-nigh inter-
changeable section of cities without remembered names, where
beneath the dark and equivocal and symbolical archways of
midnight he bedded with the women and paid them when he
had the money, and when he did not have it he bedded anyway
and then told them that he was a Negro. For a while it worked;

that was while he was still in the south. It was quite simple, quite easy. Usually all he risked was a cursing from the woman and the matron of the house, though now and then he was beaten unconscious by other patrons, to waken later in the street or in the jail. . . .

He thought that it was loneliness which he was trying to escape and not himself. But the street ran on: catlike, one place was the same as another to him. But in none of them could he be quiet. But the street ran on in its moods and phases, always empty: he might have seen himself as in numberless avatars, in silence, doomed with motion, driven by the courage of flagged and spurred despair; by the despair of courage whose opportunities had to be flagged and spurred. He was thirty-three years old.[3]

In a house on this road the victim is caught in the deadly human machinery of fate, name of Joanna Burden. Ulysses has found his Penelope; but he is no king; and she is a virgin with a vengeance. A woman of rigid Calvinist upbringing, she has denied the flesh and worked overtime in the cause of justice for the Negro. She becomes violently enamored of Joe Christmas and drags him down with her into a pit of sexual corruption. He knows that he ought to run away from her, but he is unable to tear himself away.

The innocent and the virgin are locked together, and from this misalliance damnation and death ineluctably follow. The damnation is the terrible sense of being accursed, disaster not synonymous with death, even though issuing in death. Christmas not only to get away but to defend himself against her murderous fury shoots and kills Joanna Burden. Then, of course, he must run again, but now for the last time—journey's end is in sight.

. . . he is entering it again, the street which ran for thirty years. It had been a paved street, where going should be fast. It had made a circle and he is still inside of it. Though during the last seven days he has had no paved street, yet he has travelled farther than in all the thirty years before. And yet he is still

inside the circle. "And yet I have been farther in these seven
days than in all the thirty years," he thinks. "But I have never
got outside that circle. I have never broken out of the ring of
what I have already done and cannot ever undo," he thinks
quietly, sitting on the seat, with planted on the dashboard before
him the shoes, the black shoes smelling of Negro; that mark
on his ankles the gauge definite and ineradicable of the black
tide creeping up his legs, moving from his feet upward as death
moves.[4]

Damnation and death demand expiation. It is made, violently. The destruction of the innocent, the immolation of the
victim, is marked forever in the life of the community: the
transition from innocence to guilt is as ineradicable in memory
as it was violent in act. In the scene which follows the Player
is a name for the inscrutable power which shapes the end of
Man. Joe Christmas has been hunted down and trapped by a
blood-lusting mob.

. . . the Player was not done yet. When the others reached the
kitchen they saw the table flung aside now and Grimm stooping
over the body. When they approached to see what he was about,
they saw that the man was not dead yet, and when they saw
what Grimm was doing one of the men gave a choked cry and
stumbled back into the wall and began to vomit. Then Grimm
too sprang back, flinging behind him the bloody butcher knife.
"Now you'll let white women alone, even in hell," he said. But
the man on the floor had not moved. He just lay there, with his
eyes open and empty of everything save consciousness, and with
something, a shadow, about his mouth. For a long moment he
looked up at them with peaceful and unfathomable and unbearable eyes. Then his face, body, all, seemed to collapse, to fall in
upon itself, and from out the slashed garments about his hips
and loins the pent black blood rushed out of his pale body
like the rush of sparks from a rising rocket; upon that black
blast the man seemed to rise soaring into their memories forever
and ever. They are not to lose it, in whatever peaceful valleys,
beside whatever placid and reassuring streams of old age, in the
mirroring faces of whatever children they will contemplate old
disasters and newer hopes. It will be there. musing, quiet, stead-

fast, not fading and not particularly threatful, but of itself alone serene, of itself alone triumphant. Again from the town, deadened a little by the walls, the scream of the siren mounted toward its unbelievable crescendo, passing out of the realm of hearing.[5]

Something of the epic image survives in this shattering climax. The community is forged by this and similar sacrifices ritualistically perpetrated. (In Southern culture Grimm's valedictory to Christmas is certainly litanical.) But Christmas is the hare started, harried, and destroyed by the hounds of fate, and is in nothing "representative." A destructive innocent, himself destroyed, in dying he effects a heightening of self-awareness of the community. He is not one of the beneficiaries of this process.

III

Reverend Gail Hightower, onetime pastor of the Presbyterian church in Jefferson, is an innocent in *Light in August* whose impotent longing for a life of grand action is uncompromised and unflawed by conscience. As a preacher he had used "religion as though it were a dream. . . . It was as if he couldn't get religion and that galloping cavalry and his dead grandfather shot from the galloping horse untangled for each other, even in the pulpit. And that he could not untangle them in his private life, at home either."[6]

Ineffectual as he is as minister and as person, his dreams of glory seem harmless. Indeed, in his own way he is an understanding and compassionate human being. He does what he can to make Lena Grove, an unwed mother-about-to-be, comfortable in her time of need. He listens in inexhaustible patience and understanding to Mrs. Hine's piteous account of how Joe Christmas came to be. He tries to protect Joe Christmas from the mob; just as many years ago he had stood his own ground against the threats—and one whipping—of the masked riders.

So Hightower is *not* a mere absurd nothing of a human

being. He lives on the margins. His inability to live nearer the
center of life is something inflicted on him by his own dreams
of innocence.

> And Hightower leans there in the window, in the August heat,
> oblivious of the odor in which he lives—that smell of people
> who no longer live in life: that odor of overplump desiccation
> and stale linen as though a precursor of the tomb—listening
> to the feet which he seems to hear still long after he knows
> that he cannot, thinking, "God bless him. God help him"; think-
> ing *To be young. To be young. There is nothing else like it:
> there is nothing else in the world* He is thinking quietly: "I should
> not have got out of the habit of prayer."[7]

As for the dreams of glory gone forever, he knows how
false they are, how comically faithless to fact, but he will not
let go of them.

> You can see it, hear it: the shouts, the shots, the shouting of
> triumph and terror. the drumming hooves, the trees uprearing
> against that red glare as though fixed too in terror, the sharp
> gables of houses like the jagged edge of the exploding and ul-
> timate earth. Now it is a close place: you can feel, hear in the
> darkness horses pulled short up, plunging; clashes of arms; whis-
> pers overloud, hard breathing, the voices still triumphant; behind
> them the rest of the troops galloping past toward the rallying
> bugles. That you must hear, feel: then you see. You see before
> the crash, in the abrupt red glare the horses with wide eyes and
> nostrils in tossing heads, sweat-stained; the gleam of metal, the
> white gaunt faces of living scarecrows who have not eaten all
> they wanted at one time since they could remember; perhaps
> some of them had already dismounted, perhaps one or two had
> already entered the henhouse. All this you see before the crash
> of the shotgun comes: then blackness again. It was just the one
> shot. "And of course he would be right in de way of hit," Cinthy
> said. "Stealin' chickens. A man growed, wid a married son, gone
> to a war whar his business was killin' Yankees, killed in some-
> body else's henhouse wid a han'ful of feathers. Stealing
> chickens."[8]

In his fantasy-life Hightower is forever confusing his own being with his grandfather, whose martial end was no more glorious than to have been shot stealing chickens. But for all his knowing how illusory is the image of glory, Hightower cannot resist it.

So in the end the myriad ghostly creatures of his dreams claim him.

It is as though they had merely waited until he could find something to pant with, to be reaffirmed in triumph and desire with, with this last left of honor and pride and life. He hears above his heart the thunder increase, myriad and drumming. Like a long sighing of wind in trees it begins, then they sweep into sight, borne now upon a cloud of phantom dust. They rush past, forwardleaning in the saddles, with brandished arms, beneath whipping ribbons from slanted and eager lances; with tumult and soundless yelling they sweep past like a tide whose crest is jagged with the wild heads of horses and the brandished arms of men like the crater of the world in explosion. They rush past, are gone; the dust swirls skyward sucking, fades away into the night which has fully come. Yet, leaning forward in the window, his bandaged head huge and without depth upon the twin blobs of his hands upon the ledge, it seems to him that he still hears them: the wild bugles and the clashing sabres and the dying thunder of hooves.[9]

Hightower is not quite the innocent that Sutpen and Christmas are. Cancelled by fantasies though he is, Hightower *knows* that they are fantasies. He knows also that he is guilty for his wife's sad fate—or at least that his grandfather is guilty! So complete is Hightower's identification with the past.

As he sits in the window, leaning forward above his motionless hands, sweat begins to pour from him, springing out like blood, and pouring. Out of the instant the sandclutched wheel of thinking turns on with the slow implacability of a medieval, torture instrument, beneath the wrenched and broken sockets of his spirit, his life: "Then, if this is so, if I am the instrument of her despair and death, then I am in turn instrument of someone out-

side myself. And I know that for fifty years I have not even
been clay: I have been a single instant of darkness in which a
horse galloped and a gun crashed. And if I am my dead grandfather on the instant of his death, then my wife, his grandson's
wife . . . the debaucher and murderer of my grandson's wife,
since I could neither let my grandson live or die. . . ."[10]

So even though Hightower admits some sense of guilt, he
is unable to offer restitution looking toward the recovery of
purity.

Elsewhere in Faulkner's fiction there is a man who under-
stands the necessity for restitution. He is Isaac McCaslin. He
cannot actually stem the tide of social corruption, and he cannot
singlehandedly lift the curse off the land and its people; but
these things he can do, and does, *symbolically*.

Uncle Ike McCaslin is only one of the heroes of the story
"The Bear." The bear itself is certainly one of the heroes, but
it is from McCaslin we learn about the shattering of innocence
and the meaning of restitution.

The bear and the wilderness his home are both destroyed.
Their destruction marks not only the end of an era but also
the transition from one condition of the human spirit, the transition identifiable as the destruction of innocence. This transition,
this "fall," is not accomplished in a twinkling of an eye, in a
single errant stroke. The curse is real enough, as McCaslin
says:

> This whole land, the whole South, is cursed, and all of us who
> derive from it, whom it ever suckled, white and black both,
> lie under the curse. Granted that my people brought the curse
> onto the land: maybe for that reason their descendants alone
> can—not resist it, not combat it—maybe just endure and outlast
> it until the curse is lifted. Then your peoples' turn will come
> because we have forfeited ours. But not now. Not yet. Don't
> you see?[11]

The grip of this curse upon the land and its diverse people—

Indian first, then white, then Negro—is as old as the land in human memory and possession. Lucas Beauchamp, Negro though kin of McCaslin, gives a theological interpretation of this situation.

> He saw the land already accursed even as Ikkemotubbe and Ikkemotubbe's father old Issetibbeha and old Issetibbeha's fathers too held it, already tainted even before any white man owned it by what Grandfather and his kind, his fathers, had brought into the new land which He had vouchsafed them out of pity and sufferance, on condition of pity and humility and sufferance and endurance, from that old world's corrupt and worthless twilight as though in the sailfuls of the old world's tainted wind which drove the ships . . . and no hope for the land anywhere so long as Ikkemotubbe's blood and substituting for it another blood, could He accomplish His purpose.[12]

Thus the history of the wilderness, its grim tale of spoliation, rapine, and violence both impulsive and premeditated, is but the human story in capsule: dispossessed of Eden's splendor, man himself becomes a dispossessor, taking and using what is not his for his own purposes, the same being anything but divine.

This history has a strange denouement: relinquishment, voluntary and calm. Isaac McCaslin renounces his patrimony of land, moves to town, purchases a kit of carpentering tools and so earns thereafter his meager living.

> . . . because if the Nazarene had found carpentering good for the life and ends He had assumed and elected to serve, it would be all right too for Isaac McCaslin even though Isaac McCaslin's ends, although simple enough in their apparent motivation, were and would be always incomprehensible to him, and his life, invincible enough in its needs, if he could have helped himself, not being the Nazarene, he would not have chosen it: and paid it back.[13]

Ike McCaslin's renunciation does not change the community

about him or the course of history. For that matter his own
reactions to the "taint of nigger blood" are altogether conventional as the story "Delta Autumn" makes appallingly clear.
("He cried, not loud, in a voice of amazement, pity and outrage: 'You're a nigger!' ")[14] Nevertheless, he sees the human
condition in the South as life under a curse: in a terrible kind
of innocence the people raped the good earth, "deswamped
and denuded and derivered" it. But retribution and revenge
are at hand.

> Chinese and African and Aryan and Jew, all breed and spawn
> together until no man has time to say which one is which nor
> cares . . . no wonder the ruined woods I used to know dont cry
> for retribution! he thought: the people who have destroyed it will
> accomplish its revenge.[15]

The fall from innocence brings evils in its train, but there
is something peculiarly just ("condign" is the ancient word) in
these evils; not just evil but evil somehow appropriate, as
though the cosmos had what man so commonly appears to lack:
an instinct for justice. So McCaslin believes; and so he tries
to live.

IV

Faulkner's innocents create dark mischief; and they must
endure the general ruination brought down upon good and evil
men alike; and this argues a kind of moral frame in the cosmos.

Albert Camus' version of Innocence and the Fall is so strik-
ingly different from Faulkner's at vital points that we wonder
whether they inhabit the same moral universe. We may also
very well wonder which moral universe we ought to call
"home." In Camus' story *The Fall* the image of a man who
learns wisdom by running afoul of the cosmic moral frame has
disappeared. Over the ruins of this traditional image rises the
image of man with no moral reference beyond his own existence.

Jean-Baptiste Clamence, the narrator and sole character of *The Fall,* was once a shiningly successful man: he was able to live purely and only for himself and in and for his own happiness. He found himself infinitely and unambiguously lovable in his role as a lawyer specializing in what he calls the "noble cases"—widows and orphans. So he says of himself:

> I enjoyed my own nature to the fullest, and we all know that there lies happiness, although, to sooth one another mutually, we occasionally pretend to condemn such joys as selfishness.[16]

His was life in a kind of Eden, as he says: "I never remembered anything but myself."[17] (As he says later, "For more than thirty years I had been in love exclusively with myself.")[18]

His paradisiacal self-harmony and serenity are flawed in the following way. One serenely beautiful night as he walks on a bridge over the Seine he hears a woman laugh somewhere in the dark. Later the same evening he hears laughter beneath his window; and soon thereafter when he sees his reflection in the mirror, smiling as usual, he says: "it seemed to me that my smile was double."[19] He has become aware of himself as a man for whom all of life is a series of parts or roles; and in that awareness his unity, his unquestioning and happy love of himself, is ruined; and he begins to laugh at himself. His enjoyment of himself now compromised, his egocentrism nevertheless remains intact.

> On my own admission, I could live happily only on condition that all the individuals on earth, or the greatest possible number, were turned toward me, eternally in suspense, devoid of independent life, and ready to answer my call at any moment, doomed in short to sterility until the day I should deign to favor them. In short, for me to live happily it was essential for the creatures I chose not to live at all. They must receive their life, sporadically, only at my bidding.[20]

Then the ax falls. His memory, once beatifically faulty, is restored and offers up the hour of his judgment.

> That particular night in November, two or three years before the evening when I thought I heard laughter behind me, I was returning to the Left Bank and my home by way of the Pont Royal. It was an hour past midnight, a fine rain was falling, a drizzle rather, that scattered the few people on the streets. I had just left a mistress, who was surely already asleep. I was enjoying that walk, a little numbed, my body calmed and irrigated by a flow of blood gentle as the falling rain. On the bridge I passed behind a figure leaning over the railing and seeming to stare at the river. On closer view, I made out a slim young woman dressed in black. The back of her neck, cool and damp between her dark hair and coat collar, stirred me. But I went on after a moment's hesitation. At the end of the bridge I followed the quays toward Saint-Michel, where I lived. I had already gone some fifty yards when I heard the sound—which, despite the distance, seemed dreadfully loud in the midnight silence—of a body striking the water. I stopped short, but without turning around. Almost at once I heard a cry, repeated several times, which was going downstream; then it suddenly ceased. The silence that followed, as the night suddenly stood still, seemed interminable. I wanted to run and yet didn't stir. I was trembling, I believe from cold and shock. I told myself that I had to be quick and I felt an irresistible weakness steal over me. I have forgotten what I thought then. "Too late, too far . . ." or something of the sort. I was still listening as I stood motionless. Then, slowly under the rain, I went away. I informed no one.[21]

After this, he was "aware only of [the] dissonances and disorder." He knows that he is under judgment and the punishment is laughter. "The whole universe then began to laugh at me."[22]

Thereupon he tries everything to restore the shattered image of himself as infinitely lovable: drunkenness, gambling, drugs, debauchery, but nothing availed. "Because I longed for eternal life I went to bed with harlots and drank for nights on end. In the morning, to be sure, my mouth was filled with the bitter taste of the mortal state."[23] Orgy dulled the pain for the blissful moment; but the original, the deadly wounding sin was neither forgiven nor forgotten.

> Then I realized, calmly as you resign yourself to an idea the truth of which you have long known, that that cry which had sounded over the Seine behind me years before had never ceased, carried by the river to the waters of the Channel, to travel throughout the world, across the limitless expanse of the ocean, and that it had waited for me there until the day I had encountered it. I realized likewise that it would continue to await me on seas and rivers, everywhere, in short where lies the bitter water of my baptism.[24]

No wonder that he says of the Last Judgment, "it takes place every day,"[25] and yet Judgment is simply other people, since the "world's order . . . is ambiguous."[26]

So our "fallen" creature commits himself to perdition: life in a city that is all fogs and canals, and life from which every prospect of real forgiveness has been obliterated. He can find no escape from the dreariness of guilt and self-alienation.

The Fall is a mordant parable standing the traditional image of sinner on its head. "Innocence" is the original perfection of egocentricity; and "Fall" is a chance event which shatters the hitherto impenetrable walls of the self-infatuated ego. Thus exposed to the realities of guilt, anxiety, and inability really to love another being, the role-playing counterfeit person (Jean-Baptiste Clamence is an assumed name) disintegrates.

V

If we take Camus' parable at all seriously we shall find ourselves wondering whether the dream of innocence is itself not a prime symptom of the human sickness. Perhaps the dream is but illusion, a trick played by corrupt memory or corrupt hope; and if memory and hope be corrupt shall any important part or moment of human life escape taint, distortion, and disfigurement?

If Original Sin expresses anything of power or validity to the generality of our contemporaries, it willl be as the corrupt and corrupting memory, that is: the memory in which a person cherishes an image of himself as one of the pure in heart and not merely as a happy innocent. This is the plight of Jean-Baptiste Clamence.

IV

The travail of erotic man

According to a song which once enjoyed credibility as well as popularity, love is the sweet mystery of life. It is love which makes the world go around. For many generations the word "love" itself richly hinted a magic marriage of spirit and flesh, the weight of glory inclining toward spirit. Now the magic is largely dispelled; the word is a balding cliché, and the image of man, born to love and be loved and therein, in that blessed giving and receiving, to become his true self, has been put on the rack. No longer mysterious, love is no longer monarch; and it is at best dubiously divine. "Love is not love which alters when it alteration finds"—the alteration has indeed occurred. Thereby another aspect of the Heritage has been modified, if not cancelled.

This process of modification has had two phases in our own century. The second phase does not appear to move back toward the tradition from which it was first dislocated. D. H. Lawrence is the capital illustration of the first phase. He evokes an image which breaks decisively with the long regnant tradition. It is the image of the person who discovers in fulfilled sexual love the key to fulfilled human life. Thus sexuality emerges as a divine power, and to be devoted rightly to it is to be absorbed into the mysterious life-force which creates all being. Mystic union with the Ultimate is the ultimate blessing; but the free and full expression of sexuality is the way into that bliss.

This Lawrentian image has been displaced by the second phase of modification, by which sexual love is stripped of the last shred of traditional *and* Lawrentian sentimentality. Man emerges as the creature afflicted with a strange complication: he is driven to create a fantasy-world out of copulation. So Eros is brought down from the plane of divinity, to which its claim of place was never better than dubious, into clear biological fate. Erotic man is in bitter, deadly travail: he struggles hopelessly against this fate.

II

Lady Chatterley's Lover is the principal text for our consideration of Lawrence. The sufficient reasons for this concentration are in the book itself. The tormented history of its publication and its popularity as a "purple" book are irrelevant to our purpose. Lawrence's novels breathe religious passions. Lawrence was appalled by the terrible havoc wreaked by the worship of false gods; and he had an overwhelming desire to see humanity rescued from this dire bondage and restored to its rightful creativity and holiness. In the grip of these passions Lawrence directs a prophetic fury upon the falsifications perpetrated by "Christian" civilization. This thing of demonic rigidity and power ("Conscience") has corrupted the flesh by making it a shameful thing, an object of guilt. In *The Man Who Died* he tried with desperate seriousness to free Jesus from those false gods of Shame and Guilt. Jesus' *real* resurrection occurs only when he can finally surrender himself to the freely offered body of a woman. From this blessed sexual union he learns at last what love really is, and the deadly poison of fear of the Flesh is drained off.

Another false god draws Lawrence's ire and fire in *Lady Chatterley's Lover:* the new deity of capitalistic culture which (after Henry James) he calls "the bitch-goddess, Success."[1] Connie Chatterley, the heroine, is not obsessed with this idol. Her situation relative to the god Shame-and-Guilt, is more ambiguous. She had all the advantages of a rational, thoroughly enlightened rearing; so she has a very easy conscience, if any at all, about her youthful sexual experiences. Yet when she was still in her teens she felt that "this sex business was one of the most ancient, sordid connections and subjections. . . . The beautiful pure freedom of a woman was infinitely more wonderful than any sexual love. . . ."[2] She had never known inhibition, but nevertheless she became disenchanted with sex at a very tender age. Naturally, therefore, she was deeply delighted, upon marrying Clifford Chatterley in 1917, to learn that he was not very much interested in sex. It "was merely an accident, or an adjunct, one of the curious obsolete, organic processes which persisted in its own clumsiness, but was not really necessary."[3]

In the last year of the First World War Clifford was terribly wounded in combat. He came home permanently invalid and sexually useless. Writing was the only work in which he was greatly interested. To the rest of the world, except for persons upon whom he was heavily dependent, he was unrelated. So Connie lived "in the void"[4] and became progressively restless and dissatisfied. This is her condition when Michaelis, a successful playwright, enters her life. He is a devoted slave of Success, the "bitch-goddess," who "roamed, snarling and protective, round the half-humble, half-defiant Michaelis' heels. . . ."[5]

Connie Chatterley accepts Michaelis as her lover, as much from pity as passion. She "never really understood him, but in her way, she loved him. And all the time she felt the reflection of his hopelessness in her."[6] But Michaelis is not much of a lover. Sexually he is a feverish adolescent, intimidated and outraged by her abundant sexual passion. He cannot achieve a free and full sexual relationship to her, and before long he slinks away. Other men intellectualized and verbalized all of the reality out of sex. All of them, husband included, were worshippers of the bitch-goddess and were therefore worshippers of *nothingness,* emptiness, illusion—"they were all alike, they left everything out."[7]

> Nothingness! To accept the great nothingness of life seemed to be the one end of living. All the many busy and important little things that make up the grand sum-total of nothingness![8]

She feels trapped in this condition. When she meets a real man, Mellors, the game-keeper on Chatterley's estate, she will not let herself be attracted at first. Soon she sees that there is something unspoiled, clean, powerful, and whole in him. At the same time her husband begins to see the other face of the "bitch-goddess."

> He realized now that the bitch-goddess of success had two main appetites: one for flattery, adulation, stroking and tickling, such as writers and artists gave her; but the other a grimmer appetite for meat and bones. And the meat and bones for the bitch-goddess were provided by the men who made money in industry.
> Yes, there were two great groups of dogs wrangling for the bitch-goddess: the group of the flatterers, those who offered her amusement, stories, films, plays: and the other, much less showy much more savage breed, those who gave her meat, the real substance of money. The well-groomed showy dogs of amusement wrangled and snarled among themselves for the favors of the bitch-goddess. But it was nothing to the silent fight-to-the-death that went on among the indispensable, the bone-bringers.[9]

A great lust for power is kindled in him. The deep vitalities of his unconscious flame into life. Connie sees that his life is being hideously distorted: he is becoming "almost a *creature,* with a hard, efficient shell of an exterior and a pulpy interior, one of the amazing crabs and lobsters of the modern, industrial and financial world, invertebrates of the crustacean order, with shells of steel, like machines, and inner bodies of soft pulp."[10]

Despairing of meaning in her life and world, she is driven into Mellors' arms. She turns to sex in desperation, but soon a new life of soaring passion breaks across her emptiness and despair; and for the first time in her life she is totally in love. True she is reluctant to give up "her hard bright female power,"[11] but her essential womanhood triumphs. She has entered the kingdom of the one true God, that power which makes us one with all creative life. Mellors also recognizes in himself the power of this authentic divinity, pulling him from the cold love of his own wounds inflicted by other loves. So together they learn to put shame to death, "the deep organic shame, the old, old physical fear which crouches in the bodily roots of us."[12] In this death of the old shameful Adam they find "life"!

Lawrence's moral passion commands this result: human existence comes into its own only when erotic love is delivered from gods ancient and modern which distort, corrupt, and deaden it. Elsewhere Lawrence took considerable pains to show that this renewal of life is not accomplished simply by throwing off the repressions and inhibitions of sexual moral conventions. The demands of the creative life-force can be fulfilled only in the unashamedly sexual union of a real woman and a real man, responsive to each in a mystical-sexual way. Lawrence sought to disclose, therefore, the possibility of returning to a natural-ness and wholeness of life-force, of which the symbol (if not the substance) is abundant sexuality.

I have again used the term "mystical" with some deliberate-ness. In many pages of *Lady Chatterley's Lover* the ecstasy of sexual union is given this quality of meaning: true lovers are in touch with the ultimately real, and they joyously sacrifice to it the burdensome illusions of consciously sought individuality; and thus find truth, peace, and creative power.

III

With what prophetic vehemence and grandeur Lawrence assails the false gods which debase human life so unspeakably! The industrial system, the worship of power, the meretricious intellectualism of polite society, how fiercely he hates these counterfeit divinities! How brightly burns the flame of his love for human life restored to rightful pride and power of the body! But how sad therefore that the fully authorized text of *Lady Chatterley's Lover* arrived too late in our era to seem much more than a curiosity. Too much has changed in the years since Lawrence's death. For one thing, the language of fiction and of stage has succeeded in reducing the quasi-mystical "taboo" words, with which he experimented so boldly in *Lady Chatterley's Lover,* to tedious and banal naughtiness, if indeed the sophisticated audience even takes note of them. But something more decisive than the shattering of these semantic proprieties has occurred: the image of the person fulfilled by his freely expressed sexuality has been very severely damaged. Erotic man is sick. Neither anticonventional nor conventional sexual behavior offers any real hope of cure.

William Styron has marked carefully and expressed vividly this descent of erotic man into damnation all too palpable. His novel *Lie Down in Darkness,* for this and for other reasons, was one of the most remarkable novels to appear during the decade of the fifties.

This is a story of love unstrung. Conjugal, parental, sibling, sexual, all of the forms of love are blighted, all are ruined, by forces so grim, unrelenting, and final that we cannot hesitate for long to call them, in a collective name, Fate.

As the novel opens Milton Loftis is waiting at the railroad station in a small southern city for the train bringing from New York the body of his one great love, his daughter Peyton. With him are the Loftis' Negro woman, Ella Swan (a Faulknerian figure), and Dolly Bonner, Milton's mistress. His wife, Helen, has not come to the station, and this is the first hint that nothing remains of their marriage except bitter recriminations, hungover confessions of guilt, and diseased memory.

Milton will turn out to be a pretty limp, soggy hero. Now in his middle fifties, he has never escaped the domination of his father's image; as a college student he was already a drunkard, a man "who drank not only because whiskey made him drunk but because away from his father, he found the sudden freedom oppressive."[13]

In his pocket Loftis has a letter from his dead darling. This missive is in effect her last will and testament. In it she confesses:

> Oh, Daddy, I don't know what's wrong. I've tried to grow up —to be a good little girl, as you would say, but everywhere I turn I seem to walk deeper and deeper into some terrible despair. What's wrong, Daddy? What's wrong? Why is happiness such a precious thing? What have we done with our lives so that everywhere we turn—no matter how hard we try not to—we cause other people sorrow?[14]

The novel eventually answers her "What's wrong, Daddy?" Her love for other men is all entangled with her love for Daddy, her Bunny; and her radically confused love drives her to desperate promiscuity.

> Then I would say: oh, my Harry, my lost sweet Harry [her alienated husband], I have not fornicated in the darkness because I wanted to but because I was punishing myself for punishing you: yet something far past dreaming or memory, and darker than either, impels me, and you do not know, for once I awoke, half-sleeping, and pulled away. "No Bunny," I said.[15]

In the end, as she is about to commit suicide, she soliloquizes thus:

> Oh, I would say, you've never understood me, Harry, that not out of vengeance have I accomplished all my sins, but because something has always been close to dying in my soul, and I've sinned only in order to lie down in darkness and find, somewhere in the net of dreams, a new father, a new home.[16]

On his side, Milton's love for his beautiful adorable daughter has long since alienated his wife from both of them, and it makes his relationship with his mistress, Dolly Bonner, as unsatisfactory as it is immoral.

For her part, Helen Loftis has also lived under the power of a fate: a sexual frigidity somehow tied up with the image of *her* father. She has also a relentlessly powerful, but politely disguised, hatred for Peyton as having been instrumental (so she feels) in the death of the congenitally crippled younger daughter, Maudie.

This hopelessly tangled skein of undisciplined and destructive passions is exposed in its true colors at the wedding of Peyton Loftis and Harry Miller. Everything hitherto sensed as inevitable occurs during the wedding. The ruination is dreadful, and at the same time, comic. Where, now, is the sweet mystery of life, love, that sweet power which blesses all it touches? Where now the salvatory grace of sexuality, banishing everything that impedes, distorts, or corrupts the fecund life-thrust? In this brilliantly executed scene Milton Loftis disintegrates altogether —a man never more than barely adequate becomes a full-blown incestuous drunkard—and the soul of his wife becomes a frozen wasteland; and his beloved daughter is swept into a nymphomaniacal existence with suicide as its denouement. It is but a short pace to a moral: to love is to be doomed. The creative expression of love in *any* mode is blocked and corrupted by the remorseless images of Family, Honor, Guilt, Father, Daughter, and so on.

The process modifying the image of man has indeed carried us beyond Lawrence. No longer do we believe that the original beautiful human possibility has been effaced by the industrial machine, or by the craving for power or success, or by conventional morality. The power to love is somehow flawed from the start; and thereafter it lays waste. Erotic man is a creature pursued by a harsh, consuming fate.

IV

A further stage in the decline of the erotic image as the normative representation of health, beauty, and creative power is disclosed in Lawrence Durrell's *The Alexandria Quartet*. *Justine,* the first volume, has particular significance in this connection. *Clea,* the last volume, answers questions unresolved until that point.

The heroine of *Justine,* is Justine herself, the beautiful absolutely unforgettable *femme fatale* of many conquests. The narrator (Darley) says of her:

> She could not help but remind me of that race of terriffic queens which left behind them the ammoniac smell of their incestuous loves to hover like a cloud over the Alexandrian subconscious. The giant man-eating cats like Arsinoe were her true siblings.[17]

Justine is a story of sexual intrigue. On first reading it appears that everybody either has slept or is sleeping with everybody else, which is to say that the characters in the *Alexandria Quartet* are quite beyond the reach of traditional Christian morals. The narrator already has a mistress when Justine enters his life; and Justine herself is married; and Darley's (the narrator) mistress, Melissa, who dies, has a child by another man, Justine's husband, in fact. This is indeed a sticky web; and Durrell spins it with sensuous artistry until it seems to the reader that, quite as Justine herself says, Alexandria the city is predestination, although not quite as Augustine taught that doctrine.

In all her drive Justine seeks she knows not what. Her unrelenting sexual hunger is the consequence of a violently traumatic experience as a girl; and she has been haunted in her dreams by the foul villian ever since. Eventually this image is exorcised. Justine thereafter becomes—a mere woman! Fleeing Alexandria she takes up life in a Jewish community in Palestine. Clea sees her there and reports that

> . . . having become cured of the mental aberrations brought about by her dreams, her fears, she has been deflated like a bag. For so long the fantasy occupied the foreground of her life that now she is dispossessed of her entire stock-in-trade. It is not only that the death of Capodistria has removed the chief actor in this shadow-play, her chief gaoler. The illness itself had kept her on the move, and when it died it left in its place total exhaustion. She has, so to speak, extinguished with her sexuality her very claims on life, almost her reason. People driven like this to the very boundaries of freewill are forced to turn somewhere for help, to make absolute decisions. If she had not been an Alexandrian [i.e. sceptic] this would have taken the form of religious conversion.[18]

Justine's sexual abundance actually had its roots in disease— "mental aberrations" produced by sick dreams.

Darley knows what she sought in him, and what sort of failure he himself was that made her hungry for him. He confesses that as his sexual powers declined his power of self-giving enlarged. Justine, being a woman and therefore "a natural possessive," seeks desperately to capture Darley's inner core, that part, that essence, which could only be given as laughter and friendship. So far then as Justine was concerned, Darley could see in sex merely a "terminology," a "skin-language," whose essential meaning must lie beyond itself. Having arrived at detachment through travail, Darley has really to fight Justine off. He says:

Women are sexual robbers, and it was this treasure of detachment she hoped to steal from me—the jewel growing in the
toad's head. It was the signature of this detachment she saw
written across my life with all its haphazardness, discordance,
disorderliness. My value was not in anything I achieved or anything I owned. Justine loved me because I presented to her
something which was indestructible—a person already formed
who could not be broken. She was haunted by the feeling that
even while I was loving her I was wishing at the same time only
to die! This she found unendurable.[19]

Darley says the sexual act itself is an "eternally tragic and
ludicrous position of engagement."[20] This, mind you, is the
calm acknowledgment of realities, not the disgust and disenchantment of one who, adolescent-like, has lived in illusion. To
vision purged of illusion Eros is intrigue, entanglement, con-
spiracy, betrayal, jealousy; and it is therefore the mother of
murder. The ingratiating sentimentalisms of an epoch which
has dismissed the Christian sentiments can no longer itself
conceal the truth: sex is a biological mechanism generating
diseases which destroy the real creativities of human life. How
the shade of Lawrence must weep! Whatever of the romantic
imagination is left to the rest of us must weep with him; and
something of a residual religious philosophic piety which
endows the flesh with sacramental value, does this not join
the spectral lamentation for the departed image of erotic man?

Clea, the last volume of *The Alexandria Quartet,* applies a
brake to the rhetorical flight of our despair. Clea is an angel
of light not untouched by darkness but invincible against it.
In *Justine* she is so described by Darley.

She lives without lovers or family ties, without malices or pets,
concentrating with a single-mindedness upon her painting which
she takes seriously, but not too seriously. In her work, too, she
is lucky; for these bold yet elegant canvasses radiate clemency
and humor. They are full of a sense of play—like children
much-beloved.
But I see that I have foolishly spoken of her as "denying

herself marriage." How this would anger her: for I remember her once saying: "If we are to be friends you must not think or speak about me as someone who is denying herself something in my life. My solitude does not deprive me of anything, nor am I fitted to be other than I am. I want you to see how successful I am and not imagine me full of inner failings. As for love itself —*cher ami*—I told you already that love interested me only very briefly—and men more briefly still; the few, indeed the one, experience which marked me was an experience with a woman. I am still living in the happiness of that perfectly *achieved* relationship; any physical substitute would seem today horribly vulgar and hollow. But do not imagine me as suffering from any fashionable form of a broken heart. No. In a funny sort of way I feel that our love has really gained by the passing of the love-object; it is as if the physical body somehow stood in the way of love's true growth, its self-realization."[21]

Clea has passed beyond the reach of sexual love, but not because she is a victim of moralism or of physiological or psychological defects. She is no longer a slave of sex because she has found a genuinely creative expression of her being in art and in non-sexual friendship.

The fourth part of the quartet is laid in Alexandria during the Second World War. Many things have happened to change the city; and Darley's friends have not escaped catastrophe. Justine has lost most of her beauty. Darley's onetime mistress, Melissa, is dead and is now a very shadowy memory —she was but one of the "costumes of love." As for Justine, she "had indeed been an illusionist's creation, raised upon the faulty armature of misinterpreted words, actions, gestures. Truly there was no blame here. The real culprit was my love which had invented an image on which to feed."[22] This comes home to him in perfect clarity and final force when Justine offers herself to him. That passion, at least, is all spent.

Darley has really returned to Alexandria to find Clea. When he finds her an idyllic love-affair blooms. The lovely moment is suddenly shattered by a mysterious spiritual *malaise* which overcomes Clea; and he loses her. The affliction miraculously overcome, Clea returns to Darley, and then nearly loses her life in an underwater accident caused by a harpoon gun. Darley rescues her by desperate heroics. When she is recuperating in the hospital she confesses to Darley that she has loved another man for a long time, with whom she had achieved full womanhood. Then she sends Darley away to make a fresh start on a writing career; and having herself become "a real human being," she is now also free to be "an artist at last."[23] The quartet concludes on this note.

Sexual love, then, at its best, is but a stage of the spirit on the way into the kingdom of creativity. It is not the end, the grand purpose and goal of human life. It does not offer union with the Ultimate. The inevitable suffering it causes *may* help one to come of age as a creative spirit. Unfortunately no overarching Providence guides love to such fruition—when it happens, what is there to thank but luck?

The question may sell the quartet short. Durrell seems to have gone to great pains to say that love is the terrible baptism through which the spirit has access to true freedom and power. Some do not survive the ordeal; and others have not the wherewithal—the life, the courage—to rise to it. But whatever one's theology the fact must be faced: a few make it into the creative kingdom, and many do not.

V

If Durrell holds a truthful mirror up to the present age, we should have to say that the image of man rendered most nearly divine by love is shattered, unless there is something god-like in the creation of art.

The other possibilities of becoming divine are slender, scanty, and dim. The ecstasy of sex in which self momentarily dies in the sense of union with the ultimate life-force—how remote, what worlds away, that all seems! We *know* too much about love; we have examined and explained sexuality from too many angles to be enthralled by that prospect. Moreover, the present age has relaxed beyond recall the inhibitions which impart to sexuality the grand mysteriousness, the miraculous potency, earlier ages saw in it and thereafter loved and feared it, sought it and fled from it, damned and idolized it.

Ecstasy has another, more metaphysical, defect: the flight from the curses and burdens of temporality into the time-lessness of ecstasy is foredoomed to failure so long as one still lives when the ecstasy wanes. Still living, one is oppressed by the reality of fatalities and destinies spread out on the time-line from which no ecstasy can really save and which no communion can alter or postpone. The ecstatic joys and suf-fering of sexual love may momentarily dim the lineaments of that last and greatest enemy, the Future; but this enemy has us by the throat anyway.

If we may put the issue religiously, granted that we human creatures are implausible candidates for proper divinity, what are the real prospects for returning from such preposterous fantasies to an image of man who loves the world and himself at once realistically and joyfully—a creature who learns to affirm creatureliness, a time-bound being who learns to affirm time?

VI

The latest novel of Alberto Moravia, *The Empty Canvas,* offers some tantalizing hints of return to such an image. In his earlier novels and stories (*Two Women* is something of an exception), Moravia has painted a picture of human life altogether unflattering to pretensions of fidelity, honor, and courage. He has been especially forceful in attack upon what-ever of pretty illusion about sex managed to survive until now. He destroys the *mystique* of sex with clinical precision and detachment. He has anatomized boredom, triviality, and point-lessness as coldly and carefully.

Dino, the protagonist of *The Empty Canvas,* is a painter who can no longer paint. The symptom and symbol of his essential deadness is an empty canvas on his easel. He is self-enclosed in an impenetrable shell he himself calls *Boredom:* he is unable to be related to anything outside himself. In this condition he becomes obsessed by his mistress, Cecilia: he wants to possess her absolutely, she must become a thing, an extension and implement of his own ego. But the only way he can reach her and possess her is sexually; so the sexual relation itself is reduced to frenzied copulation. He can take only, he cannot give; and in this condition he knows that he does not really have Cecilia.

In his despair Dino contemplates suicide. He is spared this fate by a nearly fatal auto accident. As he is slowly recovering in the hospital, he discovers to his astonishment that a profound change in his being has occurred. He is finding pleasure in the fact that Cecilia is away having a good time with his sexual competitor, an actor; he is pleased "that she should exist . . . in a manner which was her own and which was different from mine and in contrast with mine."[24] From this he progresses to another change.

I no longer desired to possess her but to watch her live her life, just as she was, that is, to contemplate her in the same way that I contemplated the tree outside my window. This contemplation would never come to an end for the simple reason that I did not wish it to come to an end, that is, I did not wish the tree, or Cecilia, or any other object outside myself, to become boring to me and consequently to cease to exist. In reality, as I suddenly realized with a feeling almost of surprise, I had relinquished Cecilia once and for all; and, strange to relate, from the very moment of this relinquishment, Cecilia had begun to exist for me.[25]

He now loves Cecilia in a new way, which means that for the first time he loves *Cecilia.* When she returns to him they may again be sexual partners, but his love for her does not depend on this resumption.

I had learned to love Cecilia, or rather, to love her without complications.[26]

The phrase, "to love Cecilia without complications" may strike an unpleasant note: the hopeful plea of lovers who want love only and no responsibility, no "strings." This is not what the phrase means for Dino. It means that he is now able to accept relationship to realities which have being in their own right and not as extensions of his ego. He is no longer a world, he is a being with others in the world. He has come at last into genuine subjecthood; and he may become again (or perhaps for the first time), an artist, a creative spirit.[27]

So the creative power in man awaits deliverance from the thralldom of unrelatedness. Sexual love as an instrument for breaking out of this terrible prison, is *demonic:* it but *confirms* the prison. Somehow one must learn to love "without complications." But how? For Dino deliverance comes accidentally but none the less really. I venture to say "gratuitously" rather than "accidentally," and I mean by "gratuitously" the mystery of grace, a conjunction of divine power with human subjecthood. This interpretation of Dino's saving accident clearly overreaches Moravia's novel and probably falsifies it in some significant measure. I am not so sure that it is an implausible falsification.

VII

This is not the moment just before imagination is recaptured by the traditional image of man, the heaven-blessed wanderer, the creature whose travail is ordained as the discipline of fulfillment. Heaven is not that clear nor the discipline of suffering that precious; and the race has gone down other roads at breakneck speed in abysmal darkness; and by any proper human calculation man may not be worth redemption from his self-ordained fate. I happen to believe that what man is, essentially has not and will not let us go all the way into the Kingdom of Darkness. He is what he remembers best in the moment of truth. He is also what he hopes in the moment of blessed peace from terror. He is also what he does with his creative talent when time is no longer a hateful enemy, digging at him from the guilty past and the terrible future. Of a truth he is set in this life to wander on the earth, and now into the space beyond earth. This does not mean that he is an exile, or a cast-off, or a prisoner, or a puppet, unless memory fails and hope is destroyed either by comforts too many or terrors too immense.

But what about the future? Man at his best is child of hope. Is he therefore an orphan?

V

The vicissitudes of eschatological man

The refrain of an old Finnish folk-hymn is a question: "Will not day come soon?" This question is also a refrain of civilization in the Western world. Muted by seasons of good feeling, it rises to crescendo when "terror lays waste at noonday." When terror strikes, or impends, people yearn for the Day of God when He will return to earth bringing everlasting peace to this dark, tormented, and turbulent scene. This, of course, is but one expression of an eschatological image of human existence, that is, man is a being whose fulfillment is bound into some future event in which all history, if not the cosmos at large, will be consummated. The prophets of ancient Israel forge some of the important elements of this image. They proclaim the Day of the Lord when He will summon all nations to judgment and thereafter gather the righteous into His everlasting kingdom. Christianity contributed the images of the Last Judgment, a day of divine wrath and creaturely terror when the unregenerate will descend into a hell of everlasting torment and the righteous will ascend into a heaven of eternal blessedness.[1]

These archaic myths have lost their potency except for an occasional flicker in retrograde revivalism. The eschatological image has survived in other forms—other myths, if you will. The eschatological thrust, it seems, will not be denied. The historical optimism of the modern age is an expression of this thrust. Another sterling expression is the seriousness with which time is taken, and, above all, future time, as though the essence of human life could only be expressed futuristically. Much of contemporary secular life, as well as traditional religion, bids man live for tomorrow, for the day which follows this one, and for a Great Tomorrow at the end of all our days. "There is a great day coming!" is one answer to the plaintive cry, "Will not day come soon?"

"There is a great day coming" has lost plausibility in the devastations of the twentieth century. Bygone generations believed that they could descry the skyline of the Heavenly City ever more clearly as time carried them to it. Evolution (if not God) was carrying mankind to a certain glorious fulfillment. Then the dogs of war were unleashed, twice in a generation; and the visions of the splendid City of God as our earthly destiny were once and for all shattered, except for minds unhinged by these calamities or for those constitutionally incapable of learning from experience.

The eschatological images capable of surviving have had to be therefore either hopelessly out of touch with the historical actualities, as any implausible golden dream, or hard-bitten, tough-minded, and realistic. We shall not pay much attention to the former simply because the bridge to the future is never built of such gossamer. On the other hand, the tough-fibered "realistic" images have had notorious difficulties maintaining a rational balance of optimism for the long-run future of mankind with a rigorous employment of indiscriminate means to serve an end ultimately humane. In our time the most evangelical historical optimists have been the Marxists. They believe that history moves to a grand denouement, a consummation in which man's alienation from himself will have been overcome. In the meantime, conflict, confusion, and the instrumentalities of planned terror are the order of the day.

II

John Steinbeck's *In Dubious Battle* (1936) is a striking expression of the optimistic-realistic eschatological image. It is a novel of the violent labor wars on the West Coast during the Depression. The hero, Jim Nolan, deeply embittered by his personal hardship amid the injustices of the social order, signs up with the Communist party because, as he says, "I want to work toward something. I feel dead. I thought I might get alive again."[2] He is taken on by the party and given its hard discipline. He begins to learn the uses of adversity when his mentor, Harry Nilson, tells him:

"Now we start our strike, and Torgas County gets itself an ordinance that makes congregation unlawful. Now what happens? We congregate the men. A bunch of sheriff's men try to push them around, and that starts a fight. There's nothing like a fight to cement the men together. Well, then the owners start a vigilantes committee, bunch of fool shoe-clerks, or my friends the American Legion boys trying to pretend they aren't middle-aged, cinching in their belts to hide their pot-bellies—there I go again. Well, the vigilantes start shooting. If they knock over some of the tramps we have a public funeral; and after that, we get some real action. Maybe they have to call out the troops." He was breathing hard in excitement. "Jesus man! The troops win, allright! But everytime a guardsman jabs a fruit tramp with a bayonet a thousand men all over the country come on our side. Christ Almighty! If we can only get the troops called out."[3]

It is necessary to learn how to use everything and everybody for the cause. Of course this includes the disciplined use of violence, as Jim explains to one of his colleagues, Doc Burton.

Jim said, "Y'ought to think only of the end, Doc. Out of all this struggle a good thing is going to grow. That makes it worthwhile."
"Jim, I wish I knew it. But in my little experience the end is never very different in its nature from the means. Damn it, Jim, you can only build a violent thing with violence."
"I don't believe that," Jim said. "All great things have violent beginnings."[4]

Shortly Jim witnesses and gives his sturdiest moral support to an application of violence in behalf of the Cause.

"I want a billboard," said Mac, "not a corpse. All right, kid. I guess you're for it." The boy tried to retreat. He bent down, trying to cower. Mac took him firmly by the shoulder. His right fist worked in quick, short hammer blows, one after another. The nose cracked flat, the other eye closed, and the dark bruises formed on the cheeks. The boy jerked about wildly to escape the short, precise strokes. Suddenly the torture stopped. "Untie him," Mac said. He wiped his bloody fist on the boy's leather jacket. "It didn't hurt much," he said. "You'll show up pretty in high school. Now shut up your bawling. Tell the kids in town what's waitin' for 'em."
"Shall I wash his face?" London asked.
"Hell no! I do a surgeon's job, and you want to spoil it. You think I liked it?"[5]

When Mac confesses to some twinges of sympathy for the victim, Jim rebukes him.

"Don't think of it," Jim said. "It's just a little part of the whole thing. Sympathy is as bad as fear. That was like a doctor's work. It was an operation, that's all."[6]

By now the protagonist of the humane eschatological vision is indifferent to any now-existing human values. He has a self-transcending person-destroying holy passion. Little wonder that he is able to tell the wife of one of his co-workers:

> Everything's crumbling down and washing away. But this is just a little bit of the whole thing. This isn't anything, Lisa. You and I aren't much in the whole thing. See, Lisa?[7]

In the end Jim loses his life in the conflict ruthlessly fomented for the Ultimate Cause. Immediately he is awarded the bright crown of martyrdom in this holy cause, by one of his co-workers.

> London handed the lantern up, and Mac set it carefully on the floor, beside the body, so that its light fell on the head. He stood up and faced the crowd. His hands gripped the rail. His eyes were wide and white. In front he could see the massed men, eyes shining in the lamplight. Behind the front row, the men were lumped and dark. Mac shivered. He moved his jaws to speak, and seemed to break the frozen jaws loose. His voice was high and monotonous. "This guy didn't want nothing for himself—" he began. His knuckles were white, where he grasped the rail. "Comrades! He didn't want nothing for himself—".[8]

III

Steinbeck's novel is more than a story of social ferment. It deals seriously with eschatological man. Eschatological man so imaged is a creature with a terrible duality of motivations: violent resentment of the social forces which have cheated him out of his rights; and passionate attachment to a splendid vision of an age to come when the furious conflict generated by injustice will have been resolved forever into the peace of a classless community.

Since then this eschatological man has suffered thunderous rebuke: we have witnessed and felt a violent recoil against the soul-destroying image of Marxist historical optimism. Arthur Koestler's *Darkness at Noon* (1941) is one of the most poignant expressions of this recoil.

The chief character is Rubashov, once a party functionary of considerable power but now a prisoner under indictment for political crimes against the people. He is the last of the Russian Old Guard Bolsheviks, the rest of them having died from "historical" rather than natural causes.

Between the torture and the interrogations Rubashov has ample opportunity to reflect upon his career as an eschatological man. He had been beyond the reach of feelings; he had been hard because he had believed that the party is always right. This unsullied confidence was supported by a theological doctrine—dogma, more correctly.

> History knows no scruples and no hesitation. Inert and unerring, she flows towards her goal. At every bend in her course she leaves the mud which she carries and the corpses of the drowned. History knows her way. She makes no mistakes. He who has not absolute faith in History does not belong in the Party's ranks."[9]

Now he is beset by doubts induced by memories of the things he and others had done to human beings.

> When and where in history had there ever been such defective saints? Whenever had a good cause been worse represented? If the Party embodied the will of history, then history itself was defective.[10]

Defective saints indeed! His own career had included ruthless betrayal of friends and associates, as party policy dictated: he had been beyond the reach of conscience. Indeed so complete had been his devotion to the party that he had betrayed his beloved mistress, Arlova, for the good of the Cause.

The Marxist "theology"—its elaborate theoretical justification for its eschatological brutality—he now judges in terms of its dreadful results in the present.

Acting consequentially in the interests of the coming generations, we have laid such terrible privations on the present one that its average length of life is shortened by a quarter.[11]

Eventually Rubashov signs the inevitable false confession and receives sentence of death as his expiation for sins against the people. As he awaits his executioners he meditates on the high themes of suffering and individuality. He had participated passionately in a revolution intended to abolish unnecessary suffering; but the revolution was being carried out by increasing enormously the physical hardships and torments of the present generations.

> So the question now ran: Was such an operation justified? Obviously it was, if one spoke in the abstract of "mankind"; but, applied to "man" in the singular, to the cipher 2-4, the real human being of bone and flesh and blood and skin, the principle led to absurdity.[12]

"2-4" is the code signal for "I" in the taps made on the cell walls by the prisoners communicating thus with one another.

Dimly but surely Rubashov realizes that in accepting the party's reduction of the first personal singular, the "I," to a "grammatical fiction" he had betrayed himself and all mankind. No wonder, then, that the Revolution has fallen on the evil days of absolute dictatorship! The great cause of ultimate freedom, peace and justice for all, has gone aground; once again a splendid vision of the Great Day coming has rotted out. And now, what?

But Rubashov can still dream fitfully:

> Perhaps now would come the time of great darkness.
> Perhaps later, much later, the new movement would arise—with new flags, a new spirit knowing of both: of economic fatality *and* the "oceanic sense." Perhaps the members of the new party will wear monks' cowls, and preach that only purity of means can justify the ends. Perhaps they will teach that the tenet is wrong which says that a man is the quotient of one million divided by one million, and will introduce a new kind of arith-

metic based on multiplication: on the joining of a million in-
dividuals to form a new entity which, no longer an amorphous
mass, will develop a consciousness and an individuality of its
own, with an "oceanic feeling" increased a millionfold, in un-
limited yet self-contained space.[13]

But as he walks towards the execution chamber he asks:

Where was the Promised Land? Did there really exist any such
goal for this wandering mankind? That was a question to which
he would have liked an answer before it was too late. Moses
had not been allowed to enter the land of promise either. But
he had been allowed to see it, from the top of the mountain,
spread at his feet. Thus, it was easy to die, with the visible cer-
tainty of one's goal before one's eyes. He, Nicolas Salmanovitch
Rubashov, had not been taken to the top of a mountain; and
wherever his eye looked, he saw nothing but desert and the darkness of night.[14]

So the disenchanted eschatological man is destroyed, his
once mastering vision of the Great Tomorrow has been shattered. What then is the *real* tragedy of Rubashov? His death?
Or the destruction of the rightness and beauty of the Cause
to which he had wholeheartedly sacrificed the demands of the
spirit? Are they not blessed who do not live to see the gods
whom they have served in unswerving devotion disintegrate
into stinking obscenities? Or are they more richly blessed who
do not bow the knee before *any* image promising a Great
Tomorrow to those who sell their souls to it today?

The second question suggests a recoil from the eschatological
image as such, and not merely from Marxist Man. This sug-
gestion is developed so vigorously by Albert Camus that we
may come to suspect the operation of a counter-dogma.

IV

In *The Plague* (English translation, 1948), Albert Camus
builds a powerful case against eschatological man. This novel

is an account of an Algerian city, Oran, suddenly attacked by plague. The narrator, Rieux, a medical doctor, begins by saying that the city is a thoroughly modern place:

> "Treeless, glamourless, soulless, the town of Oran ends by seeming restful and, after a while, you go complacently to sleep there."[15]

The first announcement of the plague is a rat which has come up out of the sewers to die in the streets; but even when the first human victims die, the citizens of Oran find it very hard to believe that the plague has struck.

> In this respect our townsfolk were like everybody else, wrapped up in themselves; in other words they were humanists: they disbelieved in pestilences. A pestilence isn't a thing made to man's measure; therefore we tell ourselves that pestilence is a mere bogey of the mind, a bad dream that will pass away. But it doesn't always pass away and, from one bad dream to another, it is men who pass away, and the humanists first of all, because they haven't taken their precautions. Our townsfolk were not more to blame than others; they forgot to be modest, that was all, and thought that everything still was possible for them; which presupposed that pestilences were impossible. They went on doing business, arranged for journeys, and formed views. How should they have given a thought to anything like plague, which rules out any future, cancels journeys, silences the exchange of views. They fancied themselves free, and no one will ever be free so long as there are pestilences.[16]

Swiftly the plague digs deeply into the life of the city, destroying life in incredible prodigality and disturbing whatever it does not destroy. Soon the entire city is placed under quarantine: until the plague withdraws the citizens of Oran are cut off from the rest of the world, no one can leave, no one can enter the city. The whole city has become a pest house in which each person will be tested without mercy: courage, pity, hope, and faith will be strained to the breaking point—and beyond.

Dr. Rieux throws himself into the care of the victims, even though his science commands no cure. He works without thought of his own safety. When his closest friend, Tarrou, asks him why an atheist should show such devotion to suffering humanity, Rieux replies,

that if he believed in an all-powerful God he would cease curing the sick and leave that to Him. But no one in the world believed in a God of that sort; no, not even Paneloux, who believed that he believed in such a God. And this was proved by the fact that no one ever threw himself on Providence completely. Anyhow, in this respect Rieux believed himself to be on the right road—in fighting against creation as he found it.[17]

This means that the plague is to the doctor "a never ending defeat."[18] The only weapon in this dreadfully uneven fight is "common decency," not heroism, not even love.

Thus week by week the prisoners of plague put up what fight they could. Some, like Rambert, even contrived to fancy they were still behaving as free men and had the power of choice. But actually it would have been truer to say that by this time, mid-August, the plague had swallowed up everything and everyone. No longer were there individual destinies; only a collective destiny, made of plague and the emotions shared by all. Strongest of these emotions was the sense of exile and of deprivation, with all the cross-currents of revolt and fear set up by these.[19]

Plague attacks the spirit as effectively as it destroys flesh-and-blood: the emotions also waste away.

Without memories, without hope, they lived for the moment only. Indeed, the here and now had come to mean everything to them. For there is no denying that the plague had gradually killed off in all of us the faculty not of love only but even of friendship. Naturally enough, since love asks something of the future, and nothing was left us but a series of present moments.[20]

Dr. Rieux's religious passion, his sturdy moral defiance of

the cosmic powers, reaches white heat when helplessly he watches a boy die in outrageous pain. He says:

> "until my dying day I shall refuse to love a scheme of things in which children are put to torture."[21]

The philosophical climax of the novel is achieved in a quiet conversation between the doctor and Tarrou, who has battled the pestilence at his side all summer long. Tarrou confesses that he had the plague long before he came to Oran; and he means by "plague" a bloodguiltiness every man has simply as a member of a society which has capital punishment, that is, of an established order grounded on legal murder. This is the original sin of Western civilization, and the guilt derived from it is the universal plague. For man in this condition, Tarrou says, there is but one way to peace short of death: "the path of sympathy" for any and all who suffer. In that direction, perhaps, lies true sainthood—sainthood without God.

Rieux is not satisfied with this high-minded aspiration for "sanctification." He replies to Tarrou:

> I feel more fellowship with the defeated than with saints. Heroism and sanctity don't really appear to me, I imagine. What interests me is being a man."[22]

To be a man in a plague-infested world is as high and demanding a calling as Rieux can or would acknowledge. To acknowledge this calling is to do one's duty in one's station and to do it without delusion of grandeur or hope for heavenly reward.

Shortly after Christmas the plague mysteriously begins to abate.

> The epidemic was in retreat all along the line; the official communiques, which had at first encouraged no more than shadowy, half-hearted hopes, now confirmed the popular belief that the victory was won and the enemy abandoning his positions. Really, however, it is doubtful if this could be called a victory. All that

could be said was that the disease seemed to be leaving as un-
accountably as it had come. Our strategy had not changed, but
whereas yesterday it had obviously failed, today it seemed triumphant. Indeed, one's chief impression was that the epidemic
had called a retreat after reaching all its objectives; it had, so
to speak, achieved its purpose.[23]

Now people dare again to hope, and "once the faintest
stirring of hope became possible, the dominion of the plague
was ended." Tarrou, who is the last victim, is thus really
twice a victim: he had not found the peace he so passionately sought because he had been without hope and without
hope, Rieux says, there is no peace.

Rieux's informal epitaph for Tarrou does not mean that
the sturdy doctor has at last joined up with the religious
heritage in order to have something grandly transcendent of
man for which to hope. Earlier Camus has disposed of that
function of the religious heritage by showing how a theolog-
ically conventional Catholic priest, Father Paneloux, is alienated from the comforts of those conventions by the very fury
of the plague. The time comes when Paneloux can no longer
bring himself to preach. Then, exhausted by unremitting toil
in the hospital wards, the priest himself is stricken and dies;
but not unmistakably from the plague—it could have been
some other destroyer, perhaps even the failure of faith; so
his is "a doubtful case."[24]

But *what* should one hope for? The great sustaining hope
must be for something simple and attainable, with luck, on
earth; and that is human love.

So when the plague has claimed the last victim the city
is opened to the world, and joy abounds among reunited lovers.
Rieux ponders this resurrection:

as he listened to the cries of joy rising from the town, Rieux
remembered that such joy is always imperiled. He knew what
those jubilant crowds did not know but could have learned from

books: that the plague bacillus never dies or disappears for good; that it can lie dormant for years and years in furniture and linen-chests; that it bides its time in bedrooms, cellars, trunks, and bookshelves; and that perhaps the day would come when, for the bane and the enlightening of men, it would rouse up its rats again and send them forth to die in a happy city.[25]

The "teleology" of the plague may momentarily astonish us, the hint that the plague comes both "for the bane and the enlightening of men." Let it astonish but not arouse false hopes nor seduce understanding: it means that men can learn from even the most dreadful vicissitudes how precious a thing it is to be *human*. The man of this scientific age dreams fitfully of an age to come when the worst of suffering will have been eliminated, and to what is left it will be possible to turn a medically tranquillized countenance. *The Plague* is an unsparingly accurate shock administered to such dreams. By such modern heresies as Marxism and Scientism, eschatological man is lead to forget that he is still plague-infested. He uses murder as an instrument of policy; he unleashes total war to "protect" national interests; he does not see that the instruments he has created have destroyed the end for which he created them and for which he himself was created; he has achieved a mechanical wonder of human organization now amply capable of destroying all semblance of essential humanity, the free man in a beloved community.

If we accept Camus' instruction, and Koestler's too, we shall have to conclude that the eschatological image has been hideously defaced by modern "heresies"; and health is ours by recovering the simple hope for simple human love.

This conclusion sprouts an inference: the traditional, indeed religious, eschatological images must have been long since erased by a dialectical decision of history from which there is no rational appeal. One remembers that we have entered the "post-Christian era," if some of our most highly esteemed savants and seers are right. If such is the real shape of our world we must have left far beyond the once-blessed image of man "outward-bound" to a community, a "home-land," in which God and man are everlastingly at peace, the "Kingdom of God." That image has endured its last vicissitude, then; it is a childish picture we have become too wise to enjoy, a sweet dream shattered irremediably by the harsh, jagged, and blinding world we now call home.

If these inferences are even near the mark of truth an appropriate recognition would be a requiem for eschatological man, a valedictory somewhat more solemn, and thus with less histrionics and less preaching, and somewhat more elegaic and liturgical, than any of the dismissive exercises we have so far considered. Something like this is discoverable in Alan Paton's lyrical novel, *Cry, the Beloved Country*.

V

Paton's protagonist, Stephen Kumalo, is a native Anglican priest in South Africa. The time is the present: an hour of repression, violent conflict, and destructive anxieties.

Stephen Kumalo's son, Absalom, has left the village, for only old people can live on its ravaged land, and he now lives in Johannesburg. Stephen has received a letter from a fellow cleric in Johannesburg, telling him that his sister Gertrude is seriously ill. He takes the meager savings he and his wife have managed to scrape together and goes to the great city in great fear and trembling. The city terrifies this simple soul, but he manages to find friends. He also finds his sister: she is a liquor dealer, a prostitute, and the mother of an illegitimate son. His brother has become an unscrupulous "operator." Bitterly frustrated by the treatment of the colored people, his brother has acquired the loose morals and shabby pretensions of the white masters. He schemes, conspires, and agitates for political power, but now more for himself than for the victims of exploitation. Thus native as well as white leadership has forgotten what the greatest power is: love.

Stephen's fears are amply confirmed in due time. His son

Absalom has become a thief; in the course of robbing a house, he shoots in panic and kills the owner, one Arthur Jarvis. Jarvis is the son of a rich landowner in Kumalo's home village and this is a sad irony, because Jarvis was deeply concerned for the plight of the native peoples, and now he is dead at the hands of one of them, a fear-crazed youth.

Having done everything that he can for Absalom, now under sentence of death, and for the boy's pregnant common-law wife, Kumalo returns to his village. Heart-stricken though he is, he recovers something of his sense of responsibility to his parish and village. He begins to hope that health may yet be restored to the ravaged earth upon which people must depend for livelihood. Too, James Jarvis, the father of the murdered man, is unexpectedly generous in coming to the financial rescue of the small native church: in keeping with his own wife's last wishes, he will see a new church built. So new life begins to stir in the valley.

On the evening before Absalom is to be executed in Johannesburg, Stephen goes up into the mountain to keep the death vigil. There he says his prayers: of confession; and of thanksgiving; and of intercession for all he knows, naming them one by one; and—after he had unwontedly dozed—for his son about to die; and for

> . . . all the people of Africa, the beloved country . . . God save Africa. But he would not see that salvation. It lay afar off, because men were afraid of it.[26]

When he awakes the next time, dawn is breaking; and even though his beloved Absalom may even now be dead, Stephen Kumalo hopes for another dawn, the coming of the glorious day of God's Kingdom.

> But when that dawn will come, of our emancipation from the fear of bondage and the bondage of fear, why, that is a secret.[27]

Rubashov, in Koestler's *Darkness at Noon,* wonders wistfully and forlornly whether a new day will ever dawn and a human order appear in which the "I" and the "community" are both affirmed absolutely. He, certainly, has never seen that Promised Land from any peak; and he doubts at the last that such a splendid goal really exists. Thus he is the eschatological man cancelled. Kumalo, on the other hand, enjoys a perfection of confidence in the coming of the true eschatological community: from his hilltop of suffering he thinks to see its far-off dawning. When it will *really* come is a secret of the divine counsel— *when,* yes, not *if.* Thus Kumalo is the eschatological man certified and validated: he has a hope which no eventuality— whether bane or blessing—can unseat or disqualify or demean.

Paton's hero does indeed enjoy this perfection of hope. The same may make him, unwittingly no doubt, a master of the never-never game. A master of the game—he can as easily be a child as a philosopher—never loses: his hope is *never* that dismal thing, a longing overcome by the course of actual events.

A plea can be entered in Kumalo's—and any good Christian's—defense. The object of his hope, the Kingdom of God, puts him under heavy moral obligation in the present and to persons now living; and the God in whom he hopes is the giver and enforcer of these eschatologically oriented obligations. Hence even if the hope is not fulfilled *historically* in Kumalo's lifetime, it is fulfilled *ethically* so far as he can obey the command to love even his enemies. But even if he cannot obey and accepts his guilt for this failure, the hope is fulfilled ethically. Thus the dawn of the Great Day is a secret. What one must do in the meantime is not a secret but a duty as plain as it is uncomfortable.

VI

Such is the import of this deeply affecting novel, *Cry, the*

Beloved Country. In its patient, charitable dismissal of the excuses masters give for unheeding enjoyment of privilege and reckless abuse of power, and slaves give for hatred of their masters and love of violence in defying them, it is more of a Christian homily than a novel. In its portrayal of the terrible power of fear to corrupt and destroy essential human community, and in its plea for the power of love eventually to recreate the beloved human community and for the present to endure all things for hope's sake, it is one of the most moving and eloquent tracts for the times.

Nevertheless even (especially?) the greatest sermons raise questions, and this one is no exception. Let me put the most obvious ones: What headway does such a hope make against both idealistic and Machiavellian incitement to violent revolution in the name of Justice? Has the hope for that Great Tomorrow of biblical disclosure—the appearing in glory of the perfected community—become too feeble, dim, and remote, to minister to the frenzy, terror, and "wisdom" of our age? Is the image of an old Zulu country parson keeping faith in lonely vigil with all men everywhere and always who hope for the coming of the Day too weak for us? Or too strong?

Such questions may express the conviction that the eschatological possibility is the element of Western tradition most decisively lost for the present age because it is the element most vehemently denied by what man has learned about himself and his prospects. The philosophical difficulties are not the only ones, however; and they may be the least decisive. The concrete difficulties are well known to us all: perhaps we have become afraid to hope for anything but the gift of a whole skin for the next twenty-four hours; or for a little happiness before the end. Too we remember having been tricked by false hopes. If a hope has been great its failure is correspondingly destructive—or is this "law" itself beyond suspicion? To live today that something fairer might come to life tomorrow, is one of the noblest ingredients of the spirit of man. Splendid achievements and the fairest offerings of the world are prefigured somewhere and somehow in the present, whether we are joyous or distraught. Hope is among the most precious of such prefigurations. Thus man is (and pray God may remain) the eschatological creature. Whether the Day will come soon, no one knows, but one can hope; and in the meantime seek to do things which will stand the light of day.

VII

Well, what things *will* stand the light of day, whether they be done from anxiety or from simple-minded serene conviction that the mightiest power of the Universe swerves not nor changes in its moral governance?

William Faulkner answers a question something like this with the figure of Mink Snopes. Mink makes a striking conjunction with the traditional image of the Heaven-guided wanderer. He undergoes a good bit of a character transformation through the triology which begins with *The Hamlet,* runs through *The Town,* and reaches home in *The Mansion.* At first encounter Mink deserves his name: silent, unprincipled, and deadly. For the Snopes part, one must have encountered the unforgettable breed already in Faulkner's world to know what an unlovely sound it is. Its head, Flem, is unrelentingly and cunningly committed to possessing the earth, and through *The Town* seems destined to do so. Therefore other Snopes must be eliminated to further his own designs; and this shows a fine instinct for impartiality in ruthlessness. Mink is one of the Snopes marked for removal. When Mink kills a man by shooting him in the back from ambush, Flem deliberately fails to use his vast influence to get Mink off. So Mink is sent to the state prison for a long stretch; and whenever the possibility of parole for his eminently good behavior in prison begins to develop, Flem engineers its ruin. Therefore, Mink becomes as much a man of purpose as Ulysses: he lives to return to Jefferson and requite justice upon the head of his perfidious cousin, who has come into monarchical power and wealth. After many years Mink wins release from prison and at once begins his odyssey. Faulkner displays his great powers as a storyteller in making Mink's journey at once sure of consummation and suspenseful in every important phase; for through every setback and temptation Mink perseveres. He knows that Old Moster (his name for Heaven's mysterious King) will neither release nor betray him until justice is done. How then could Mink fail to prevail over every mortal power with such great faith?

> I don't need to worry. Old Moster jest punishes; He don't play jokes.[28]

At the last, when Mink has finally reach Jefferson, now almost entirely unfamiliar to him, and tracked Flem into his magnificent and ill-gotten mansion, Old Moster threatens to let him down: Mink's $7.50 pawnshop revolver misfires on the first shot and for a desperate moment Mink wonders whether he is a victim of the cruelest cosmic prank conceivable. But on the next pull of the trigger, the secondhand instrument of divine justice fires, and Flem dies with a look of final acceptance of his fate and its justice on his face. His earthly mission thus fulfilled, Mink scampers aimlessly away from the mansion, altogether free to lie down and die whenever he wants. The mother earth is ready to receive him and he is ready to give himself up to her who finally claims all her creatures for herself and sees to it—O! beyond any doubt, dissent, or declination— that they are

> . . . all mixed and jumbled up comfortable and easy so wouldn't nobody even know or even care who was which any more, himself among them, equal to any, good as any, brave as any, being inextricable from, anonymous with all of them: the beautiful, the splendid, the proud and the brave, right on up to the

very top itself among the shining phantoms and dreams which are the milestones of the long human recording—Helen and the bishops, the kings and the unhomed angels, the scornful and graceless seraphim.[29]

Earth to earth? Indeed, yes; but more, too. Even the lowly Mink Snopes becomes an image of the human community, which is one human "substance" in guilt and in righteousness. To requite the evils done to man, so conceived, is a high destiny; and his accepting it transforms a "mink" into a human being in full standing, alongside of and equal to the beautiful, the splendid, etc.

So there *is* something to be done besides "all the unnecessary bother and trouble" of grubbing and scrounging for a living and worrying about how long the good luck will last and then about being able to stand bad luck; and worrying about going to Heaven and about there not being any Heaven to go to, only Hell instead. And there is something to be done besides wondering how long the sexual ecstasy will last and whether anything as good will take its place, such as writing novels or painting pictures or organizing Little League clubs or Junior League bazaars or chairing the Board of Vestrymen. And there is something to be done besides—whether in addition to or apart from?—hoping that everything works out for the good. Injustice must have a clear rebuke, action not just words. The sufferers need care, whoever they are and whatever they suffer from. The dying need comfort, whoever they are, and no matter that some of them deserve death, for who doesn't?

This is of course a random sample of things to be done (besides tending the shop and craving ecstasies and lighting candles and saying prayers). It is a strange and wonderful fact that there are things to be done which we can do—whether we draw them at random or they descend randomly upon us —in which the human community is augmented even if our puny budget of strength and time is diminished. With the lowly Mink Snopes we discover that no one *really* travels alone no matter how aimless, erratic, and dizzy the course adopted. Above us "Old Moster" rules undeviatingly. Beneath us the earth, an ample patient equalizing grave, waits to receive us. On all sides we are accompanied by the splendidly various traveler-pilgrim, Man. *He* is the proper subject of every novel. From every great novel we come away having learned to love this woeful wonderful creature a little more, a little better. This is one reason, and a good one too, for calling some novels great.

VI

Death and transfiguration

The fate of the traditional image of man is sufficient warrant for saying that symbols "participate mortality": they live for a season and then die. The season of their life may span generations, even centuries, through which their power over imagination is so great that eventually men believe that these symbols "participate eternity" and in their proper enjoyment they have a taste of the joy of heaven. Then the season of life mysteriously ends and even the most lordly symbols fade away.

This is the way an epoch ends. Its master images lose their power and the imagination seeks other lords. The end may not be dramatic— some worlds die with a bang and others with a whimper—but any way the end does come for every system and phase of culture. And whether or not the end is really dramatic some value inheres in the dramatic metaphor, "the death of the gods." "Gods" here signify the master images of culture. Omitting the theological reality of gods, as we do here, we have nonetheless to observe that the death of a god is a

shocking event. It is a terrible disaster for the imagination and
the heart, a crisis fraught with the most formidable consequences
although it may not be reported as a crisis on the front pages
of the newspapers. When the gods die the imagination in which
they have ruled loses direction and content. The heart, whose
health depends upon having an object to love above all others,
must find another god or perish. So driven it may take false gods
unto itself. Thereafter the human spirit trivializes itself, dis-
sipating its precious energies upon random details of being
and thin aspirations.

The aimlessness which ensues upon the death of the gods
ought not to be confused with an interest in small affairs. The
latter trivialize the spirit only when no principle is available
to relate intelligibly small affairs to the great world beyond one's
doorstep. The gods, the master images, have such a function.
When they die life hitherto ordered by them begins to disintegrate.

The reduction of a master image to a stereotype is the way
a god dies. The life of an image is its expressiveness, its efficacy
as a conveyor of meaning or as an instance of meaning. The
death of an image is the fading out of its meaning, leaving
behind only a thin weak formality, a mere trace: a stereotype.

So the gods die. It is tempting to seal them in their tombs
with the profound saying, "once dead always dead," were such
wisdom itself separable from stereotype. And were it really
wise, given that fate beyond death which may properly be called
transfiguration. Transfiguration is the infusion of new meaning
into a barely extant formality. What has been a largely lifeless
convention is thus restored to life. The new life is more than
the old one but it is also an inheritor of the old. The form is
recognizable—if it were not, an entirely new thing would have
appeared—but it has been revalued; and the new value has the
vividness, definiteness, and efficacy to become a god. Thus
transfigured images are the threads of continuity between epochs
of a culture, and sometimes between different cultures. As such

they are the essential medium in which a heritage is transmitted. Indeed transfigured images are part of a heritage rather than external agents imported for its transmission. They are "time-binders," unifiers of time and experience. They are lords and gods fully ordained for their tasks in the native realm of the imagination.

II

The heritage of Western culture is heavily Christian: many of its gods have a Christian history, they participate in the historical reality of Jesus Christ. Traditionally Jesus Christ is both normative humanity and God Himself come to earth to save mankind from its just deserts. The traditional representations of this being, Jesus Christ, include cross, chalice, dove, fish, lamb. These representations began as emblems in the primitive Christian church and eventually became fully developed symbols, each uniquely expressing the value of Jesus Christ. But their being Christian has not exempted these images from the laws of the imagination. As gods generally they have come and gone; and returned transfigured; and died again; as though they were bound to a great wheel of life-and-death or were subject to a mysterious rhythm of ebb and flow governing all creation. This rhythm is one of the fundamental laws of the imagination.

The master images of Christian stamp had hardly emerged in power and glory before their attenuation began. Thrown by their own evangelical zeal against philosophically sophisticated paganism, the Christian apologists translated the biblical message into the conceptual schemes of the Hellenistic world. The biblical images began to die in that very moment, that is, they began to lose their primitive biblical value.

This Hellenization of the Gospel has sometimes been interpreted as a disaster early and inexplicably descended upon that tender lovely *naif*, the primitive Gospel. A double error is thereby committed: the historical error of supposing that the

Gospel might have been preached intelligibly to the pagan without Hellenizing it; and the philosophical error of supposing that the most primitive form of the Gospel is necessarily the moment of its greatest power of truth. We wish devoutly to avoid both elements of error and mean therefore by speaking of "Hellenization" merely to call attention to the rapidity with which the biblical images are transformed in the context of Hellenistic culture. The Cross, for example, represents the efficacious self-sacrifice of Jesus Christ for the deliverance of man from the thralldom of Sin and Death and the participation of the faithful in this offering; thus the Cross is the symbol of obedience in life and death to the will of God the Father Almighty. But the temporal immediacy of the Kingdom of Glory was diminished by the passage of time and the necessity of coming to terms with Rome, the ruler of the world here below. In the course of the conflict with Rome, the Cross became the symbol of martyrdom. When Rome fell before the barbarian, the burden of imperial civilization fell upon the Church, and the Cross became the emblem of a new empire at once spiritual and temporal. *In hoc signo* the other kingdoms of this world were threatened with destruction unless they came under the yoke of Christendom. The Cross of the "pale Galilean" had indeed overcome the world. The world had also overcome the cross of the New Testament.

According to their several necessities, the Christian generations since have religiously preserved the emblem of the cross and used it to express things not felt as real or important by the other generations. Perhaps the strangest of these transformations is the use of the cross to identify a person as: (1) a clergyman; or (2) a non-Jew. In either instance the emblem seems to have become something between an amulet and a fraternity pin.

The death of a biblical image is a way of talking about the conversion of its meaning from something vivid and compelling to something trite and weak. Its return to power and clarity, whether or not one takes it to be a miracle, is always more than the repristination of the (presumptively) original value.

Thus the persistence of a linguistic habit, or of a conceptual system, by no means guarantees a symbol-continuum uniting the present and the past. I do not discount the possibility of some real bond of unity by saying that the bond is not likely to be an identity of symbolic value. St. Paul, for example, lived in a world which long ago ceased to exist. Biblical images have died and have been transfigured many times since his world expired. If a law higher than the law of the imagination determines an identity of meaning linking his mind and ours, we shall not be able to find it by ransacking the imagination. The imagination considered by itself is a story of gods coming to be and passing out of being, of passage from richness to poverty.

III

The Fall is one of the lords in the imagination of Western man. The formality of the office extends over a rich diversity of actual office-holders. For some people (very few, I suspect) the Fall still conveys a sense, greatly dimmed relative to earlier epochs, of a fatal accident forever separating man from a condition of being in which human life was purely, spontaneously, and everlastingly good. For the rest the Fall has other meanings more or less detached from the biblical origins though not necessarily by any conscious intent. But a common meaning seems to run through the gamut of symbol transformations: the Fall is an image in which the inexpugnable reality of history is expressed. Man's being *is* his career in time. His career is the woeful wonderful passage from Innocence through Damnation and out toward fulfillment.

We should expect to find great differences in the representation of the moment and the condition from which man falls— that moment just before history begins. For instance, in Genesis it is a moment of paradisiacal simplicity and beauty; and yet was not the destroyer of Paradise, Pride, already insidiously working? St. Augustine's answer is clear enough.

The wicked deed, then,—that is to say, the transgression of eat-
ing the forbidden fruit—was committed by persons who were
already wicked.[1]

The great theologian has no real answer to the question how
this inner fall came about, that is, why Adam turned away
from a Good absolutely perfect. That is a mystery unrelievable
by any human speculation. It is a particularly bothersome
mystery for one who believes that man has a natural (created)
propensity for the good, an orientation which derives directly
from the perfect will of God Himself. Nevertheless St. Augustine
is not deterred from believing that the moment before history
begins is the moment in which love of self crowds out the love
of God.

This interpretation of the biblical Fall has long been normative in Christian reflection, and in one feature or another it is
still largely accepted by many theologians. I cite it here as a
capital illustration of the death of an image and its transfiguration. Genesis itself has nothing of St. Augustine's profound
inward-spiritual speculation. In Genesis Adam breaks the
clearly stated and clearly heard Law of God; and by God's
mercy as well as His wrath, Adam lives to suffer the consequences, as do we all. St. Augustine's Adam inwardly plots
rebellion and is therefore bound to sin outwardly. In this he
is all mankind, man as such prefigured. We learn nothing from
Genesis about Adam's natural propensities and less than nothing
about agitations among the angels which adumbrate Adam's
fall. Perhaps St. Augustine's Adam was planted by St. Paul;
but St. Paul's Adam is already a transformation of the Adam of
Genesis; and St. Paul does not seem to know nearly as much
about Adam's interiority as Augustine does.

In any case the Fall was launched long ago on what has
turned out to be a remarkable career. In the modern world
it becomes a defining characteristic of the novel. The hero falls
from Innocence, represented commonly as virginity. He be-

comes a creature of guilt and is alientated from his native condition. In this process he learns what life is all about and what he is. In the end he is a man richer in wisdom for all his suffering. So he is carried toward reconciliation with reality even though his sins may not be entirely forgiven. His fall, then, can be seen as fortunate (*O felix culpa!*): his seduction (or rape) yields a greater good than he would otherwise have attained. I do not mean that the master novelists have taught us to expect a sure and happy release from Damnation. One thinks of Anna Karenina in Tolstoy's masterpiece and of Milly Theale in James's *Wings of the Dove*. If we have come to count on a sure and happy release, we have surely come a long way down the slope from those heights bathed in such marvelous interplay of light and shadow. We have in fact been stuffed with popular literature in which reconciliation (returning home) *is* the comfortable assured outcome. The sinner (in all likelihood an unhappy adulterer) is reaccepted provided that he is unusually diligent in cultivating the fruits of repentance and is doggedly resolute in overcoming subsequent temptation. The sinner is not supposed to believe that he or anybody else has now a better grasp of good and evil, is in any way a better and richer human being. Actually he is less a person, he is forever stained. The faithful wife, on the other hand, is a better person for it all, because she is faithful, forgiving, and righteous altogether. Perhaps in her favor we ought to modify the generalization and say that she is really better off because of another's fall.

The Fall, in other words, threatens to collapse into inane stereotype. A god has become a tedious triviality, the image of the Fall has itself fallen! Even the Fallen Woman has become a cliché—perhaps by sheer multiplication of the species—if not a joke.

It is the more remarkable, therefore, that Camus adopted the Fall for the work we considered in chapter three. Again Innocence is destroyed. Again a soul becomes a guilt-haunted homeless wanderer, a weary wraith in a dreary land. But this fallen man is very different from the first Adam: Clamence fell from the sublimity of self-adoration, of nearly flawless egocentricity, into the absurdity of self-loathing and self-flight.

The Fall is not therefore an ironical inversion of Christian verities. Camus gives us a transfigured rather than an inverted or reversed symbol; and it therefore goes beyond the ironical intention even though ironical elements are in it. The kind of luminosity and vividness Camus imparts to the Fall evokes a new world in which man is irremediably guilty *but guilty in, for, and by himself alone.* He is no longer judged and condemned by heaven's God or by a conscience in touch with an ideal order. He is self-judged and self-condemned. The Fall has become the passage from the bliss of self-ignorance to the ultimate damnation of self-knowledge—to know oneself truly is the ultimate curse.

That new world is not yet entirely visible. Even in prospect, though, it contains Damnation beyond the dream of even Camus' wretched Jean-Baptiste Clamence. It is a world in which the Fall becomes the descent into inauthenticity, that daytime nightmare of Martin Heidegger's evocation: the mode of being in which "They" become the norm and "I" abdicates sovereignty, surrenders its freedom for the specious comforts of life in the all-determining human social mass.

This version of the Fall is rather more intelligible to us in the present world than the fall of Adam traditionally represented. Heideggerian self has no divine prehistory, no Almighty Father. He is exposed altogether to powers and nullities which threaten in every moment to obliterate him, and finally do so. We can understand when this self is so badly frightened by the world that he surrenders his essential freedom and all grasp of truth for the precarious enjoyment of illusory comforts. For freedom is a dreadful burden, if it means that a man is absolutely responsible for himself and can really and finally be only what he is prepared to resolve to become. To fall backwards away from so vertiginous a prospect, to faint into the safety of the socio-biological matrix of human life, is a choice any sensitive soul can understand and be tempted to duplicate.

There are other presentments of a new world for which the Fall remains an important symbol. I instance William Golding's novel, *Free Fall,* as a different presentment.

Samuel Mountjoy, the central character and first-person narrator of this novel, has but one all-commanding question: "How did I lose my freedom?"[2] He knows that

> Somewhere, sometime, I made a choice in freedom and lost my freedom.[3]

So he seeks to recover that moment, to come back again upon that corner which, once turned, somehow determined everything. But why does he want to recover that moment in which he fell? So that he may at last understand what happened and claim it for his own—claim it, actually, as himself. From such penetration of the reality of the past, forgiveness does not necessarily come. It is possible to know oneself as being unforgiveable.

> Nothing can be repaired or changed. The innocent cannot forgive.[4]

The innocent one is Beatrice, his onetime mistress. He had loved her but not in freedom. Therefore his love for her was her destruction, and for this he endures unassuageable guilt. He has not been immobilized by this terrible burden. He has become a very successful painter, and he has other grounds as well for being happy. Nevertheless he must claim his own being. He must not only acknowledge that he chose necessity rather than freedom, but he must also recover the moment in which he did so.

> I want to understand. The grey faces peer over my shoulder. Nothing can expunge or exorcise them.[5]

Once again the Fall takes on meaning which is a continuant of the heritage only in superficial respects. The re-charged image is an embodiment of a new world. It is a world in which forgiveness is inefficacious even when people trouble to ask for it. It is a world in which people are driven to bizarre extremes to find viable substitutes for forgiveness: anaesthesia, addiction, obsession, violence against self or others—these are some of the substitutes. Each is a refuge and a fate of the damned, the *unforgiveables.*

IV

Damnation is the fate of the fallen man. Damnation is another image which dies and comes to life in striking variety.

The word itself is an echo of a past world in which it expressed a dreadful reprisal at life's and the world's end for every sin against Divine Majesty. Now the echo is very faint. Where Damnation lives at all brightly, it signifies internal states of the person rather than relationship to objective realities such as the divine righteousness. To be damned is to be inwardly stricken ("agenbite of inwit"), such as feeling life to be a hopeless burden, or having the sense of being alone in a dark silent universe. And this is to say that Damnation has traveled a long, torturous road from the biblical world, where it carries the sense of exile, that is of being cast out from the essential community of life. There it has also the sense of richly merited punishment from which there is no appeal and no time off for good behavior.

But in the Bible itself striking changes begin to occur. In the New Testament, Damnation here and there gives off the lurid glow of an apocalyptized Hell. The geography of the spiritual life begins to intrude, and one can see how it might well become all-conquering, as it does in the Middle Ages. Then Hell becomes the bottom level of a three-storied cosmos;

it has its own landscape, government, stratified citizenry, and time. The Kingdom of the Damned—frightful demons and all their prey—is as real for the people of the Middle Ages as the life on earth and heaven above. Life in the dark kingdom is beyond all possibility of relief or redemption. Light has lost all its generative power.

Men who really believe that such a hideous realm yawns greedily for victims at their very feet may well think twice before doing the things for which God will commit them to that horrid pit, and they may well sleep badly after doing them.

Devout Hell-fearers are still among us, I have no doubt. They are several worlds behind. They have not yet caught up with one of the most interesting worlds, demonically speaking, to arise since the Middle Ages, namely romanticism. In this intriguing world the damned are very important citizens. No longer denizens of a geographical Hell fixed there in torment forever for sins against God, they are people condemned to endless misery in this world for the unspeakable crimes which held inexhaustible fascination for romantic spirits. *La belle dame sans merci* is such a haunting presence, a damned soul but also a woman of infinitely seductive allure. If she is an object of holy pity and aversion, these high virtues of the beholder are flawed by his powerful craving to enjoy her even if it costs him his everlasting bliss. And then there is the Byronic hero who is determined to taste all of earth's good and evil even at the risk of damnation. If this unslakeable cosmic appetite draws Damnation down upon the hero he will embrace it with integrity, that is with bravado.

Today this hero of Damnation would be unbelievable as a contemporary. Such behavior would strike us as being adolescent, affected, tinny, and compulsive. As for *la belle dame sans merci,* she has degenerated into that indispensable stock character of contemporary fiction, the sick nymphomaniac. O how the mighty are fallen!

Judgment nearly as harsh falls upon much more recent recruits to the Legion of the Damned, the Lost Generation of the First World War, such as Lady Brett Ashley of Hemingway's *The Sun Also Rises* (1926).

Brett Ashley is surely one of the damned. She knows it, her pals know it, we all know it. She is not star-crossed or heaven-curst but is simply at hopeless odds with her self and her world. She is sexually promiscuous, but hardly for fun. Homeless by virtue of a talent for infidelity, she seeks she knows not what. In her own way she is principled: some things she will not do because, as she says, one cannot be a bitch all of the time. The satisfaction she derives from such rare episodes of self-denial may be all that restrains her from total self-destruction.

The Lost Generation did not all go on the bum in Europe after the Great War. Some of them managed the "return to normalcy." They came home to conventional marriages, and had children, and worked at jobs, politics, and occasionally, at religion. But in their own way they fared badly too: theirs was a quiet nonhistrionic, non-Bohemian damnation. (They throng the stories of F. Scott Fitzgerald and of John O'Hara.) The burdens of "normal life" are of course too much and too small for them, and so they seek anaesthesia in alcohol, sex, etc. But as the damned go they are rather ordinary people; medieval demonizing and Byronic posturing are gone altogether, leaving not a trace either of brimstone or opium in the air. The stale musk of pointless adulteries mingles with ginny belches to create an atmosphere in which *la belle* wouldn't have a fighting chance on her best night.

The ancient damned are much more interesting people, all told, than the Lost Generation. They did not fumble the world away or try to sleep through it. They sinned boldly enough, in all conscience, and not that grace should the more abound. Fortunately for our self-esteem as moderns, Damnation has not yet run its course. Eugene O'Neill, Franz Kafka, and Thomas Mann have brought forward new recruits.

Under O'Neill's treatment the company of the damned swells to appalling inclusiveness. Lost! all lost! On O'Neill's representation man is floundering in the bottomless sea of self-deceit, self-pity, and self-hatred; and there is no blessed shore anywhere in sight. Man is a pilgrim but he is neither outward bound on a mission as ennobling as perilous, nor homeward bound full of honor won in great conflicts. So this is a damnable world, but who will give the damn? Who cares that much except as a gesture of disgust or frustration? To be born in such a world is to learn early to weep for oneself and to desist therefrom only when exhausted. Not even a vagrant wisp of hope blows across such a world—only fools waste breath on hope. Perhaps the least tolerable folly, in such a world, is to love wisdom.

Kafka created a fearsomely luminous image of the modern (or is it simply the human?) world; and this image is *The Trial* (English translation, 1937). His hero is so preternaturally universal that he has an initial rather than a name: K. K is more nearly a relationship than a subject in himself; that relationship is guilt. His guilt is unnameable, not because he has committed a crime too outrageous even to be whispered, but because no being appears to divulge K's real situation before the law. Therefore he is free to become his guilt simply —and what a devastating fate thus overcomes freedom! This he does. Metaphysically and otherwise he pours his substance into the hopeless task of establishing his innocence. He necessarily loses in this undertaking, and therefore he dies "like a dog." When heaven is empty and humanity is indifferent, death is a brute episode signifying nothing.

Doctor Faustus (1947), Thomas Mann's *summa theologica,* appears to return to the medieval vision of Damnation. A *summa* must of course include the demonic, and Mann's device for its inclusion is the Faustus image; but Mann has significant modifications of the tradition to propose. The traditional Faust contracted with Satan for an empire for himself: illimitable power, endless plunder for sensual and intellectual enjoyment; and all at the price of being pelf of Satan in the life to come. Adrian Leverkühn, Mann's Faust, does not strike a bargain with Satan for a sensualist's paradise or for power to know all mysteries. He would scale the heights of creativity as a composer. He craves a god-like power and is willing to sell his soul to have it. So when he achieves this power he knows that he is damned. Then he learns to his horror that the Devil does indeed drive a hard bargain: he takes the life of Leverkühn's darling Nepo, the beautiful boy, whose terminal suffering is so frightful that Leverkühn nearly loses his mind. Then is this not ancient Faust still? Do we not sense in every Faust a cosmic conflict between ultimate evil and divine righteousness? Does not Faust always traffic with the demonic powers and thus incur the wrath of God?

To the extent that thaumaturgy figures significantly in Mann's Faustus, there is reason for giving affirmative answers to such questions. But we must note that Mann represents his hero's thaumaturgy as an obsessive dabbling in ancient superstitions unlikely to stir the sleeping dogs of Hell. Good gray Serenus Zeitblom, Ph.D., the narrator, may believe that there are demonic powers outside the Id, but does Mann really encourage *us* so to believe? I think not. Given the religious orientation of Adrian Leverkühn, creativity of the highest order is *hybris* and is certain to bring damnation as its consequence. But this offense also brings forth beauty so splendid, so exquisite, that the human spirit can scarcely endure it. Must we not say therefore that Leverkühn dares the harshest fate, Damnation, for the enrichment of man? Or did he really aspire for a kind of absolute mastery, after all, and thus lunge beyond the set boundaries of finitude? If he did the latter, he did indeed traffic with Satan, and superstition be damned; and his art is the most beautiful flower on a vine that also produced that abomination of desolation, the Nazi wickedness. Mann more than hints such a connection.

So Damnation's life has been composed of many deaths and many transfigurations. Many in our time will wonder whether that life has not finally dried up, whether, particularly, Mann's *Doctor Faustus* is not a heroic failure to make an image live for a world in which existence itself is more persistently threatened with pointlessness than with anything diabolical. The commonplace character of such damnation not only robs the image of its indispensable vividness, but also threatens it with such universal application as to make it, itself, pointless as a representation of the human condition. Can we be sobered by threat of damnation if we are all gripped by it already? If nothing can be done about a predicament so inclusive, determinative, and final, where is the merit in fixing attention upon it? "Truth for truth's sake" is a sound principle, as well as a glittering slogan, only if error is avoidable or the mind caught in it is reformable. By the same token, "we are all damned" is intelligible only if acknowledgment of its truth modifies the absoluteness of the truth it proclaims—as though "all men are damned" is true only if "some men are more damned than others" is also and more true.

Damnation has very seldom been represented as the ultimate and absolutely inclusive fate, but not simply for the reason just cited. There is also the fact that the heritage includes the image of Expiation. This image is an historically potent expression of a world whose moral governance metes punishment for crime but also includes expiation through suffering.

V

The line between Retribution and Expiation is as difficult to draw as it is important to observe. The satisfaction demanded by the moral universe may not be at all reformatory; it may be ordered and exacted simply to balance the books. On the other hand the ultimate powers may have a reformatory interest; they may want the harmony of the world restored, or perhaps even enhanced; and so they may authorize suffering to bear this value. The suffering so authorized may be that of the innocent rather than of the transgressor alone.

Expiatory suffering may be so harsh that the divine powers appear to be driving for retribution only—an eye for an eye, a life for a life. Such seems to be the situation of Orestes in the tragedies of Aeschylus. First he is made to serve as the instrument of divine vengeance against the adulteress and murderess who happens to be his mother. But thereby he becomes the object of a divine vengeance by the foul Furies, who hound him savagely over the world lusting for his blood. Finally the horrid avenging spirits are placated by Pallas Athene, who assures them that Orestes did only what the gods constrained him to do; and she promises them that if they relent they shall be installed as the incorruptible guardians of the righteousness of the city. Thus the case laid against the house of Agamemnon is lifted. The ancient quarrel of outraged blood is ended. Full satisfaction has been made.

The Eumenides is a remarkably clear instance of the transfiguration of an image, here the image of divine retribution, the Furies. In the beginning of the drama they are described as "foul," "lewd," "loathed alike by men and the heavenly gods." They represent the primitive right of blood vengeance: when blood is spilt, especially the mother's, they are unappeaseable by anything but the blood of the transgressor. Under Athene's persuasive civilizing power they become the guardians of the city's peace. The conversion is beautifully illustrated in one of their closing speeches.

> This is my prayer: Civil War
> fattening on men's ruin shall
> not thunder in our city, Let
> not the dry dust that drinks
> the black blood of citizens
> through passion for revenge
> and bloodshed for bloodshed

be given our state to prey upon.
Let them render grace for grace.
Let love be their common will;
let them hate with single heart.
Much wrong in the world thereby is healed.[6]

Judas Iscariot pays for his unspeakable sin by taking his own life. His transgression is so foul, and his self-punishment so terrible and prompt, that the relationship linking the one to the other seems purely retributive. Yet his suicide *is* a self-punishment which, given the biblical world, cannot possibly absolve his guilt. In fact it adds crime to crime to reach a horrid sum, and Judas becomes a prime figure in the Legion of the Damned.

But of course Judas is a figure in the encompassing story of Jesus Christ. Jesus Christ is everything that Judas is not. True, Judas goes beyond that story to become the image of the archtraitor, while Christ becomes the supreme image of Expiation for the sins of others. And of course the supreme symbol of Expiation is Crucifixion. Here the one perfectly righteous man suffers ultimate outrage, and his suffering is ordained to be the divine instrument of human salvation.

Christ's expiatory death includes a factor of retribution, as theologians interpret it. The righteousness of God demands satisfaction for the sins of mankind; this is offered up by Jesus Christ, the man without sin. From this transaction of sacrifice divine power is released for the reconstitution of human reality if not of the cosmos. So in the end, if not absolutely, God's interest in suffering is reformatory: the will of God is reconciliation to his righteousness rather than final damnation.

The life of the Cross has been subject to the mysterious ebb and flow which we have called the fundamental law of the imagination. In our time it has not fallen away altogether into cliché and thereafter into desuetude. In fact one of the most distinguished of our contemporaries, William Faulkner, was unable to relinquish the crucifixion image of expiation. Joe Christmas, for instance, of *Light in August,* dies in expiation for the dual crimes of being (presumably) a Negro and a murderer. As every good Christian lyncher knows the law can take care of crime number two but never of crime number one. His death becomes part of the ineradicable memory of the community, but it has no reformatory power. And of the death of Thomas Sutpen we have to say that in it he reaps the consequences of his own folly. These two, therefore, will not qualify as representation of Expiation after the Christ model. Ike McCaslin is somewhat nearer, since his renunciation of his patrimony in the land is a gesture toward the ultimate righteousness whose justice has been outraged by human rapacity and folly.

Thereafter Faulkner made two attempts to give a closer reading of the Christ model of Expiation: Temple Drake in *Requiem For A Nun* and the Corporal in *A Fable.*

If Temple Drake is unconvincing in her turn toward the expiatory life, it may be because we learned too much about her in her earlier appearance, *Sanctuary.* On the other hand we may be hard put to it to believe in a character who is so profoundly impressed and persuaded by the moralistic preachments of lawyer Stevens. What is not unbelievable is that a Temple Drake should try to rectify her moral accounts and become a better person. She may not make it all the way to Jesus but she will try.

The Corporal of *A Fable* (1950) is patterned after Jesus with excruciating attention to details: a dozen disciples, a demonic Tempter, a Judas, and an execution including the modern equivalent of a crown of thorns—an informal circlet of barbed wire. The Corporal's death is briefly efficacious: it is related to that mutual and spontaneous cessation of fire which is part of the legend of the First World War. But not as the cause thereof, rather as the effect, since the High Command must find a scapegoat and must thereafter get the war started up again. So the expiatory death does not alter the course of history by reforming the human constitution. Its efficacy is the light it throws on the eternal, time-binding conflict of good and evil. The deathless avatars, Christ and Caesar, contend with each other throughout time. But no matter how fierce the holocaust, the human spirit will prevail.

A Fable is a profoundly disappointing novel. The refurbished image of the expiatory Christ fails to take hold. Part of the reason for this may well lie in Faulkner's endowing mankind with an invincible will to prevail: such a creature does not need and can hardly benefit from the sacrifice of Jesus Christ, Son of Man and Son of God. But there is another difficulty: the original Christ is part of the total divine operation by which human life is sanctified, that is, by which unity and holiness are conferred upon it. One suspects that holiness is supernaturally difficult to make intelligible and real to the contemporary world, which has enough trouble with unity. Perhaps this is why the failure to impart luminosity to the Christ image is a pervasive one rather than Faulkner's alone. For that matter his Christ is far more plausible than the Christ of such religious tableaux as Lloyd Douglas' *The Robe*.

VI

Of all human prepossessions the dream of Sanctification is surely one of the strangest, since it suggests a primordial divine-human community in which man was altogether righteous, his every appetite being infallibly oriented upon the good.

Unkind as history has been to this dream, its imagery persists. Even when the "memory" of an antecedent condition of perfection has atrophied, images of Sanctification live on in the imagination. I propose several illustrations of this phenomenon, of which the first is Sophocles' Oedipus.

Oedipus is transformed from being a curse into a sanctifying presence. In *Oedipus Rex* he makes the great gesture of Expiation for his crimes against the gods: he puts out his own eyes and exiles himself forever from the city of his kingship, Thebes. Perhaps the gods will be satisfied by this dreadful suffering and restore health to the afflicted city. Sophocles does not say so but the hope is not unreasonable. In any case the ultimate justice of the cosmos seems to have been vindicated.

In the beginning of *Oedipus at Colonnus,* we learn that since his self-banishment from Thebes Oedipus has wandered on the earth as a blind beggar whose very name is abhorrent to all decent god-fearing people. He has not been given sanctuary by any city or person: because he is an offense to the gods he ought to be loathed and scorned by mankind. But now this attitude is rebuked. Oedipus proclaims his innocence in the dreadful crimes of parricide and incest. He admits that he killed his father but he says that he did so in self-defence and in ignorance of his father's identity. In ignorance as profound he had married his own mother, Jocasta. His terrible suffering must therefore have a providental salvific value. Accordingly he is given sanctuary at Athens. The future greatness of that city is thereby assured by the gods who have administered Oedipus' case. From his example the generations to come will learn how rectitude is esteemed by the highest gods; and Oedipus stands forth, even as he disappears in a terrifying event, as a sanctifying presence.

Sanctification in the New Testament is a condition of spirit made possible by perfect obedience to Jesus Christ. The sanctified man has achieved that perfection of mastery over flesh and ego which renders him a pure channel of divine love. Thanks to the power of God the Spirit, this condition is attainable by living persons in the conditions of this life. Eventually the church moved all its saints to heaven; but even then the saint is hailed as a saint because in heaven as on earth he is a rich blessing to a mankind forever beleagured by Satan, stupidity, and death. So here and/or hereafter the saint is a person who has achieved *purity* as a channel of divine love.

This might be instructive to an age which will not forswear the everlasting reliving of the loss of innocence.

The traditional saint of New Testament inspiration remains a figure in the spiritual landscape, but—apart from traditional piety—he has receded into the dim background as other forms of Sanctification have come to the fore. Indeed contemporary saints make strange bedfellows—if the metaphor is not too offensive—with all the saints of Christian elevation. For our age has a great fondness for the unconventional saint.

Some of the traditional saints had to overcome, in the grace of God, unsavory—as they felt—beginnings: from their own imbibing they knew how poisonously sweet were the sins of the flesh. But of course they gave up all that when the Holy Spirit claimed them for the service of God. The saint of the unconventional life, to the contrary, affirms rather than renounces the natural goodness of life in and after the flesh. His sanctifying presence is directly related to his power of affirmation of the natural life. He castigates the austerities of the spiritual life, especially as these are enjoined by men who plan to get it all back in heaven. The life of rigorous self-denial, inhibition, etc., is diseased. Therefore this modern saint does not dream of redeeming society, his quarrel with it is not a lover's quarrel. Since he aspires to destroy whatever falsifies, cheapens, and degrades the natural potentialities of the concrete individual, he attacks the precious conventions through which society as such exists. His presence therefore is hardly sanctifying to the inauthentic souls cowering behind these conventions hoping that Providence will crown conventional virtue with real gold.

In our time the unconventional saint forswears the life of the political revolutionist. The revolutionist is a slave to a scheme of human perfection achieved by political manipulation; and for this he may become a veritable hero of self-denial; but he may also become a veritable monster of tyranny over the lives of others, not hesitating to use every trick of deceit and instrument of violence—in the cause of human perfection!

The artist appears to have the highest degree of plausibility as the unconventional saint, if we conceive the artist to be the truly creative and the really free spirit. The saint in any case cannot be a mere sensualist or "materialist"—anybody can manage to espouse and practice those creeds. So the artist as saint does not live to eat, drink, copulate, or make money. When he does any of these things, he does them freely; and when he refrains from doing them, he refrains freely; and in both cases he is free from the bondage to conventionality. He attacks the "normal" validities and velleities of perception and response, but not as an adolescent hell-raiser. He will not allow the threat of Hell to obstruct or distort the free expression of individuality.

But where is this saint to be found in contemporary literature? Camus lauds him in *The Rebel*; but the artist in *The Plague*, Grand, is a pathetic joke. He is not to be found in Hemingway, or in Faulkner. And in real life, as we like to think of it, the artist is sometimes a triumph of ego-assertion, a man who creates a private world by using a private language so that his grand critique of the conventional life in an illusory world fizzles out into self-reflective crochets, and freedom descends into irresponsibility.

Moreover the sociological pessimists may have persuaded us to believe that Organization Man is beyond Sanctification. This creature has heroes, no doubt—Cary Grant, or Stan Musial, say—but his heroes lend only an illusion of vicarious glamor to a dull and pointless existence.

The sociological jeremiads underline the extent to 'which *community* has been absorbed into a massive all-devouring *society*. Such a monster is unsanctifiable and unsanctifying. Having destroyed essential human community, it throws up pseudo gods to be loved and obeyed—Success, Security, Popularity, Sexual License, etc. Although the divinity of such gods is pure illusion, the desire and hope invested in them, and the frustration and despair reaped from them, are real enough. Thanks to the limitless technical power of our world frustration and despair can be tranquillized, and the craving for freedom can be explained away. So again Sanctification is threatened with the final death, and precisely at the central point: *the power to love in and for the essential human community*. And so far a case can be made against the likelihood of a return to power of any image of Sanctification. For the sanctifying power in human life is love. Love inverted is truly demonic, whatever one makes of traditional imps of Hell. It follows that if love cannot be sanctified, all is lost. The contemporary scene offers formidable impediments to the representation of love either as sanctified or sanctifying.

Love represented as a power driving upwards from the dark underground roots of the psyche is one such impediment—a view of things roughly Freudian. But a spirituality which has been alienated from the depths of the psyche quickly becomes an expendable sentimentalism. Thus the saint represented as a triumph of spirit over flesh and as a paragon of selfless concern for the well-being of others falls into the pit of irrelevancy. Christ himself becomes a symbol of the unreal and exorbitant demands of the spirit against the flesh and the world and moves into the thin dim life of sentimentality.

D. H. Lawrence saw this and responded with characteristic passion. He offered an antidote in *The Man Who Died* (1928). He pictures Jesus as assailed by that inveterate enemy, dread of the flesh. Even after the first Resurrection Jesus is really alive because he is still victimized by that ancient enemy—he is still a virgin. An abundantly sexual woman, a pagan priestess, delivers him from the death-grip of that enemy.

> He crouched to her, and he felt the blaze of his manhood and his power rise up in his loins, magnificent.
> "I am risen!"[7]

In this way Jesus is sanctified. Does he then become a channel of sanctifying power, does he indeed become the Savior? He begets a child with the priestess who has been the instrument of his true resurrection. But who are his spiritual progeny? The Laurentian free soul? We have already seen how severely history since Lawrence has dealt with this spiritual child; more harshly, really, than the outraged piety of Lawrence's critics could have expected, but not altogether to their comfort. Nevertheless his struggle was not absolutely futile. For our own age he is a warning against fresh incursions of the black gnostic shadow against the natural goodness of the body. The saint, who crucifies the flesh because he is afraid of it and in his fear endows it with demonic potentialities, is a victim of that invasion and ought to be so identified. He at least has not overcome the alienation of human life from itself, of which the conflict of spirit and flesh is one cardinal expression; and he cannot therefore be an authentic image of Sanctification. Sanctification is a demand that human life be unitary, that is, that it be made one by the power of love which reconciles all differences.

Using such a notion of Sanctification, we can form an estimate of several late contenders for sainthood in the ranks of traditional piety.

Graham Greene created a remarkable figure, the whisky priest of *The Power and the Glory* (1940), as a representation of the hunger for sanctification. He scampers gracelessly from the pursuing zeal of the Mexican lieutenant charged with rounding up and executing recalcitrant priests. He longs for that supernatural state of grace in which love of God, love of others, and love of self are miraculously united—the true sanctification; but he stumbles drunkenly into the situation in which martyrdom is thrust upon him rather than embraced with courage, dignity, and hope. He is a confirmed alcoholic; he has fornicated and has a child to prove it; he is a craven coward who does not hesitate to lie to save his skin—altogether he is an unlikely postulant for traditional sanctification. But with God all things are possible. In spite of himself and contrary to his own view of himself, he may yet be a blessing to many. He did not die very bravely; but Greene shows how the saint-making distortions of history are already occurring almost before his body has cooled off.

The whisky priest is an ambiguous figure. He neither renounces the flesh nor affirms its natural goodness. Nothing redemptive or sanctifying is manifested in his wretchedness of guilt for his sins. Clearly, he needs the unifying love of a "beloved community." If he is the channel of such love, if he exercises its authority, Providence is indeed mysterious.

Sarah, the heroine of *The End of the Affair* (1951) is not a much clearer case. Again, she is a party to that most irresistibly symbolical sin, adultery. Dull as this affair seems to me it obviously means a great deal to her. Otherwise her grand renunciatory gesture is without meaning. This gesture is a covenant between God and herself: she will give herself to Christ if God will restore life to her lover, dazed, as it turns out, rather than mortally wounded by a German buzz-bomb. Her lover quickly recovers, Sarah keeps her part of the bargain, and she is on the road to sanctification, old-style, more or less. Unlike the whisky priest she becomes a vehicle of divine healing power, now to a stricken child, and eventually (who will doubt it?) to the soul of her erstwhile lover, who learns that he cannot compete successfully with Christ for the love of his erstwhile mistress.

I doubt that Greene intends his story to be a morality simply, a warning against the joylessness of sin, although it does seem to me that his sinners rarely have a very good time of it. He says, I take it, that the fundamental conditions of this world are (in actual sum if not coherently) a disfigurement of life; wherefore the world is a natural and implacable foe of joy whether it be sought in licit or illicit loves. But it would follow from this that the real saint, as distinguished from avatars of sanctification left over from some long-gone world, must give off light, lucidity, and joy engendered in the union of love for this world and his vision of a world-to-be to which the present world is drawn. The real saint must not be a prodigy of renunciation, because he who renounces the world must see more evil than good in it and feel himself to be unequal to its massive power and cherish something of himself as too precious to be lost in the world's manure and rubble. The saint must affirm rather than renounce the world; and to affirm it is to rejoice in its simply being there, rather than to praise it as a step to something higher and holier. Greene's people are constitutionally unable to do this; and not even grace empowers them to do it.

Two of T. S. Eliot's people enter the lists for sanctification. One of these is Harry Monchensey of *Family Reunion*. Harry is summoned to a quest for the light whose author is surely God. He has lived a joyless, guilt-haunted life among illusions. Indeed when he first appears in the play his mind is guilt-clouded on a fairly important matter: had he pushed (and not merely wished) his wife over the ship's rail to her death? His guilt is so severe and ambiguous that he is pursued by those foul avengers from the ancient world, the Furies. As he moves from these terrible shadows toward the springing light of truth and self-acknowledgment, the Furies are transformed into ministring angels. He is not yet sanctified when the play ends, but he is on the way. And the same divine power of love will set to rights everything else that is dark and crooked in the Monchensey family. Thus the "reunion" is a transforming return to the life of grace.

Celia Coplestone in *The Cocktail Party* is a much more fully realized saint. She comes into this high estate through the ministry of a psychiatrist of nearly divine powers, Sir Henry Harcourt-Reilly. Celia is a virginal soul who comes to see that the well-tempered life of English upper-class Christian gentility is not for her. This is not because one cannot really be a Christian in that way. God demands one thing of this person and another one of that person, and he has something special in mind for Celia. She gives up resisting her vocation and goes out to Africa to preach Christ. There she meets a terrible, blessed death as a martyr and becomes a sanctifying presence: although in heaven now abiding she will ever be a verdant blessing here below.

Celia is a poignant gesture toward a lost world. She is an evocation of love spiritualized to the highest degree, but she is also an exercise in nostalgia. Unfortunately for some of our contemporaries Sanctification is not brought into solider relation with reality by making her a whore rather than a virgin, the whore with the heart of gold who exorcises the evil spirits by taking the victims into her generous omnicompetent bed and who supports every liberal cause from the largesse proffered by her cash customers. No, neither the virgin nor the great-hearted whore will do. Neither exemplifies that love which makes body and soul, self and other-self, God and man, real and creative unities. Perhaps Celia fails for other reasons, too, but these may cast a sorrier light upon the world than upon her. A world able to see only footless idealism wedded to mental illness in the ultimate of self-sacrifice somehow seems not worth the blood of martyred saints. Perhaps they, who seem unalterably intent upon leading lives relatively decent, largely dull, rarely lucid, and habitually joyless except for "kicks" artificially induced, deserve such a world. The trouble is, when the saint fades out, the sinner loses intelligibility and shortly becomes a stale cliché; and the world is left to those who lack the courage to be a saint and the vividness of appetite to be a sinner.

VII

Sanctification is an image intimately related to the renewal and purification of the essential life of a community. In every disaster, whether of privation or prosperity, which befalls the community, and beyond death itself, the life in it looks to Resurrection and thereafter to Sanctification. *Resurrection is the miraculous renewal of the community. Sanctification is the reunification and purification of the powers of life thus restored.*

So understood Sanctification unites (reconciles) life and death: life is habituated to the contingency of death; death is habituated to the necessity of life. Sanctification is therefore an ultimate image in which man's finiteness is expressed and celebrated. But it is also an image of the divine community in which life and death are reconciled.

VIII

Death is one of the reigning powers in the imagination. Its demands upon the spirit are nearly as great as those levied by life itself; and its assaults upon faith, hope, love, and courage, are too well known to need review here. Therefore hardly any task could be more forbidding than to bring Death within the form of Sanctification. Yet the task is unavoidable. If it is burked or bungled, existence falls into the most radical alienation from the world.

Efforts to encompass Death in Sanctification fall into three options, the first of which is the *denial of death.*

On the face of it no project imaginable could have a worse prospect for success than the denial of death. Since everybody dies no one can expect to profit from the denial of so universal a fate. But the profit in view is not a successful outcome of a quarrel with a biological fatality; it is a condition of the spirit men call *peace.* Peace is the end in view of the traditional doctrines of immortality, and these are so many denials of death. They agree on several major points: (a) the soul has a much higher value than the body; (b) a higher value cannot be destroyed by a lower one; (c) were the soul to die the rationality of the cosmos would be impugned, which *ex hypothesi* is impossible. These convictions taken together constitute a projection of the blessed and foreordained unity of the human spirit with ultimate reality. In fact they make the human spirit one of the ultimate reals.

This view of human life has often been supported by meta-

physical arguments against the reality of the physical world.
It is a view which may express an exalted ego-evaluation im-
pervious to any qualifying shock administered by the world.
I am not concerned here with attacking the projection either on
metaphysical or psychological grounds. Rather I want to ask
whether Sanctification so represented does what it is supposed
to, that is, unifies the diverse and contentious components of
human existence. Explaining away the reality of death is a
project which threatens the goodness of existence just as existence is given, and I contend that the unity of existence must
not be purchased at the cost of that goodness. The peace projected cannot be so good that the more primitive goodness
should be jettisoned for it. In fact peace so envisaged, loved,
and craved, is responsible for much that is specious in the
present world. I confess that nothing seems more specious
than the image of man, the pure soul imprisoned in a body
disposed to sin.

Love of death is a second option for encompassing death
in the form of Sanctification. Aspects of Freudian theory, rather
than metaphysical exercises, are commonly summoned to support this option. The ghastly experiences of population-murder
in this century of course converge upon psychological dogma
to make the option persuasive.

This fatal love was explored in depth by Dostoevsky. In
The Possessed he charges nihilism with being an irreformable
love of death. On his representation this terrible love is compromised by the utopian dream of human perfectability—a
Sanctification to be achieved by scientific reason. Even there
a love of death is at work; and there as elsewhere it is a love
which springs from the will of the self to be God, to be, which
is to say, the absolute arbiter of life and death; so Kirillov kills
himself to prove that he has this god-like power.

The Freudian aspect has, I think, largely supplanted the
imagery, if not the views, of Dostoevsky, at least in the quasi-
literate mind of the age. In the Freudian account the craving
for death is a project for peace: it is the peace of the womb-

life rather than the peace of absolute nullity. In the womb the Ego has not yet emerged—to say nothing of the Super-Ego. Biologically the self has achieved differentiation from the mother, but this has not produced conflict of wills. So the mother womb is the perfect circumambient environment. Life is reduced to the encompassing and perfectly adequate nourishing Mother and the unbrookably demanding Self.

In stupified incredulity we ask why such a condition of being should be given such bizarre idealization—a condition in which the self is barely more than an alimentary canal uncomplicated by self-awareness. The answer is clear and commanding: because postuterine life denies peace in any other deeply satisfying and enduring mode. Harshly abused by the world into which we are ushered by the unforgivable trauma of birth, we carry with us the inextirpable memory of that blessed peace; and often symbolically seek it, waking and dreaming; and perhaps on the grimmest of all possible days put hand to lethal implement to win it again and forever.

So imaged, love of death is obviously a project for unity. The unity projected diminishes self-differentiation to zero in favor of a seamless continuum of gratification. It also annihilates creativity. The creative thrust carries the self toward suffering, not away from it; and this because it calls for the highest refinements of the powers of awareness and for the highest achievement of freedom. Thus creativity is the most potent challenge to the love of death: it disrupts the unity and peace projected by that love.

In its own way the love of death quarrels as bitterly and ruinously with the primitive goodness of existence as the denial of death. It is a quarrel with life itself, perhaps even with the mysterious source of all being, not the womb but God. The love of death is a projected flight from life and a denial of the goodness of existence and a fatal distrust of the world, near and far, because it contains hurtful things.

Affirmation is the third option relative to death. Death

affirmed is death incorporated in its own meaning in a form of Sanctification. This means that man has access to full human existence only through death. His most notable achievements are possible because of his mortality, not in spite of it. The human past is the achievement of persons who died and whose death is not a merely adventitious item in the flux of time: how they died and for what are part of the significant past, they have a reason, a place in a providential scheme. And so also for future time: the future is significant now so far as one is able to project things which will stand the test of death, that is, not whether they will endure forever but whether we can love them with joy though they and we sometime perish from the earth.

The affirmation of death is also the affirmation of the human community, the unity of self with other selves, as providentially ordered to human fulfillment. Such a unity is apprehended and expressed only in the images of hope. Under the conditions of existence in the world this unity is always threatened by conflicts controlled only by *ad hoc* decisions or by exhaustion or outright destruction of the warring factions. Even when peace prevails in the great public world, as among nations, the self is torn between the fear of being subsumed by some other self and the desire itself to be lord over others. Real unity is impossible either in the peace of serfdom or in the peace of lordship. In both conditions death is exalted far above its proper degree: to a slave death is overweeningly tempting as blissful release, or as an instrument of revolution; to a lord death is overweeningly tempting as the supreme instrument for enhancing and preserving power. So real peace is butchered and lunatic imposters reign. But not forever. That is hope. It is great hope only when the great peace is envisaged with love, and the great peace is this: when men no longer have good reason to hate one another as reciprocating causes of human impoverishment, for that by which one is diminished, serves to diminish all.

Such are the way of Providence. (The very word is a curse

to those who must live on scraps and refuse and hear the happy few confuse Providence with the luck of the draw.) Human community is indissoluble. It is one in the enjoyment of the primitive goodness of existence, and in guilt and hatred, and in the hope for Sanctification beyond which no relapse into destructive conflict is conceivable.

Providence is inseparable from the idea and the image of election. Increasingly, I think, we must apprehend election to mean the *personal* obligation to realize the human possibility, which is to participate in the humanization of the protohuman creature each man is in the beginning. To be human is to apprehend a good which suffering and death help to define. But they do not help automatically or instinctively. One must resolve to make something of their brute factuality, for they will not make themselves to be anything but just brute factuality. The powers of imagination; and the powers of love; and the powers of endurance—forbearance, patience, and hope; all are called for, all can enter the lists to create a human good which is not spoiled or effaced by suffering and death. Indeed such inclusive and maximal effort must be made if human existence is ever to be more than sound and fury with rare intermissions of lucidity, peace, and joy.

Sanctification stands forth, then, as the hope for the full humanization of the human creature. That does not seem too much to hope for. But man is a singular creature. He can be undone by the misfiring of his own purposes. His purposes can misfire because he wrongly envisages the good. He can wrongly envisage the good because he can tell persuasive lies to himself and live with and love even the most violently distorted images of himself as if they were perfect expression of truth. Other creatures have perished because Nature played cruel pranks with climate, food, predators, etc. Man alone has been endowed with the ambiguously valued talent for tricking and lying himself into oblivion.

IX

Why then should we wonder at the preoccupation of the present age with the Image of Man? The stress of crisis, public and private, is much too great and complex to write off this obsession as narcissism. Moreover, the preoccupation with the human image does not seem to be part of a sweeping humanistic revolt, such as the Sophist movement in Hellenic culture in the Fifth Century B.C., or the Renaissance. At the moment we should have the greatest difficulty making out any comparably concerted or lucid attack upon dehumanizing forces in our culture. There are these forces; and they do come under attack; but the attack splutters fitfully and generally lacks unity, depth, and direction.

So the preoccupation with the Image of Man has more wistfulness than fury; as though we could only await passively the next outrage against the human community and hope somehow to survive it.

The wistfulness is produced by the degradation of once normative dogmas and images. Bereft of these one is obliged to choose something from somewhere. In this "freedom" people seem to turn more frequently and more longingly to the arts than to science, religion, or philosophy, hoping there to find the image which they can embrace without nausea.

Shall the blind lead the blind? Has God appointed the artist *per se* to be prophet, priest, judge? Artists search as avidly as any for the really normative images, except where they are content to fall back, nostalgically, upon the finality of the heritage and thereby bend Time into a magic wheel. As we know, the novelist particularly is an interpreter of the human condition. To execute this purpose he needs both a "point of view"—an angle of vision—and definitive images. On the whole he seems to be in the common trouble at this point. Is the present age such poor material as all that? Or is creative imagination under eclipse?

There are many people who write well: they can plot scenes, and manage dialogue, and project character—especially downward into the Freudian jungle. But they seem not to know what to make of the world; and so the worlds they conjure are meretricious, they fail of humanization. What will eventually appear in this situation to give center for a reorganization of the imagination, and thereafter of the will, I cannot even guess. I am sure that something will: unless we have lost the human possibility forever, there will be a rebirth of images.

Notes

CHAPTER II

1 One of Faulkner's characters expresses this beautifully when he thus relates himself to the past of his community: "I dont hate it," Quentin said, quickly, at once, immediately; "I dont hate it," he said. *I dont hate it* he thought, panting in the cold air, the iron New England dark; *I dont. I dont! I dont hate it! I dont hate it! (Absalom, Absalom!* [Modern Library Edition; New York, 1951]), 378.

2 For a fuller discussion of "factualism," see my article, "The Theological Situation after Fifty Years," *The Yale Review,* LI (Autumn, 1961), 75–101.

3 (Modern Standard Authors Edition; New York, 1949), 191.

4 *Ulysses* (Modern Library Edition; New York, 1934), 5.

5 In the beautiful ironical *Portrait of the Artist as a Young Man* he had already explored art and aestheticism as "faiths" alternative to Catholic Christianity. Stephen Dedalus there appears as a youth of exquisite sensitivities who sees himself as a grand artificer, a creator of epic dimensions self-appointed to be the "forger of his race's conscience." This is a peerless portrait of a young man's glorious illusions.

6 *Ibid.,* 14.

7 *Ibid.,* 12.

8 *Ibid.,* 566.

9   *Ibid.*, 567.
10   *Ibid.*
11   *Ibid.*
12   *Ibid.*
13   *Ibid.*, 22.
14   *Ibid.*, 104.
15   *Ibid.*, 723.
16   *Ibid.*, 336.
17   *Ibid.*, 336.
18   *Ibid.*, 339.
19   *Ibid.*
20   *Ibid.*, 38.
21   *Ibid.*, 166-68.
22   *Ibid.*, 238.
23   *Ibid.*, 240.
24   *Ibid.*, 236.
25   *Ibid.*, 721-22.
26   The phrase is R. W. B. Lewis', from his book, *The Picaresque Saint* (Philadelphia and New York, 1959).

CHAPTER III

1   *Absalom, Absalom!* 263-64.
2   *Ibid.*, 288.
3   *Light in August* (Modern Library Edition; New York, 1950), 195-97.
4   *Ibid.*, 296-97.
5   *Ibid.*, 406-407.
6   *Ibid.*, 53.
7   *Ibid.*, 277-78.
8   *Ibid.*, 424-25.
9   *Ibid.*, 431-32.
10   *Ibid.*, 429-30.
11   "The Bear," in *Go Down Moses* (Modern Library Edition, New York, 1942), 278.
12   *Ibid.*, 258-59.
13   *Ibid.*, 309-10.
14   "Delta Autumn," in *Go Down Moses*, 361.
15   *Ibid.*, 364.
16   *The Fall*, trans. Justin O'Brien (New York, 1957), 20.
17   *Ibid.*, 50.

18   *Ibid.,* 100.
19   *Ibid.,* 40.
20   *Ibid.,* 68.
21   *Ibid.,* 69-70.
22   *Ibid.,* 78, 80.
23   *Ibid.,* 102.
24   *Ibid.,* 108.
25   *Ibid.,* 111.
26   *Ibid.,* 113.

CHAPTER IV

1   Lawrence had a strong sense of intimate relationship linking these two false gods. He does not always succeed in making this sense sufficiently clear to his reader. Some may suppose that Lawrence would have been assisted into adequate clarity on this connection, by a better knowledge of Freud; and perhaps N. O. Brown's *Life Against Death* would—had it been available—have shown Lawrence that the love of Money (filthy lucre) must be interpreted anally, excrementally. Anal fixation and sexual inhibition may thus be but two aspects of one inclusive torment of the psyche. For my part I do not suppose that Lawrence would have achieved the requisite clarity by such an appropriation of Freud; but that is because Lawrence was already committed to realizing his *own* imagery (mythology, if you will) and to have borrowed Freud's (rather more obviously mythological) could only have further confused the *aesthetic* achievement. Brown's anal image is his own poetic creation, and it would be more plausible if it were given a Broadway mounting.

2   *Lady Chatterley's Lover* (New York, 1959), 14.
3   *Ibid.,* 11.
4   *Ibid.,* 18.
5   *Ibid.,* 22.
6   *Ibid.,* 32.
7   *Ibid.,* 59.
8   *Ibid.,* 63.
9   *Ibid.,* 125.
10   *Ibid.,* 128-29.
11   *Ibid.,* 161.
12   *Ibid.,* 298.

13 *Lie Down in Darkness* ("New American Library" [New York, 1952]), 17.
14 *Ibid.*, 47.
15 *Ibid.*, 481.
16 *Ibid.*, 484.
17 *Justine* (Giant Cardinal Edition; New York, 1961), 11.
18 *Ibid.*, 247.
19 *Ibid.*, 200.
20 *Ibid.*, 189.
21 *Ibid.*, 127-28.
22 *Clea* (Giant Cardinal Edition; New York, 1961), 47.
23 *Ibid.*, 275.
24 *The Empty Canvas,* trans. Angus Davidson (New York, 1961), 305.
25 *Ibid.*
26 *Ibid.*, 306.
27 Moravia's appropriation of a kind of existentialist resolution seems to me substantially more persuasive than a similar movement made by Styron in *Set This House on Fire* (New York, 1959). Styron's hero, Cass Kinsolving, is saved from the death which would have been an "out" from total moral degradation, by the sheer fact of existence: reduced to this sheer datum he clings to it for his salvation, and he *is* saved. Dino, on the other hand, discovers *something existing in its own rightful being*—a tree he sees from his hospital bed in the first instance, and then his mistress; and he comes to affirm, and not merely acknowledge, these existent beings for what they are in their own right.

CHAPTER V

1 A proper historical account of eschatological patterns would make much of the Iranian contribution to Christian apocalypticism. Iranian religion has proved to be a very hardy perennial, in fact. The persistently garish, and occasionally bizarre, qualities of latter-day "Christian" apocalypticism (e.g. Jehovah's Witnesses) are indications of this.
2 *In Dubious Battle* (New York, 1961), 6.
3 *Ibid.*, 22.

4 *Ibid.*, 184.
5 *Ibid.*, 198.
6 *Ibid.*, 199.
7 *Ibid.*, 227.
8 *Ibid.*, 250.
9 *Darkness at Noon*, trans. Daphne Hardy ("New American Library" [New York, 1956]), 36.
10 *Ibid.*, 46.
11 *Ibid.*, 115.
12 *Ibid.*, 181.
13 *Ibid.*, 185.
14 *Ibid.*, 188.
15 *The Plague.* trans. Stuart Gilbert (New York, 1957), 5.
16 *Ibid.*, 35.
17 *Ibid.*, 116.
18 *Ibid.*, 118.
19 *Ibid.*, 151.
20 *Ibid.*, 165.
21 *Ibid.*, 197.
22 *Ibid.*, 231.
23 *Ibid.*, 243.
24 *Ibid.*, 211.
25 *Ibid.*, 278.
26 *Cry, the Beloved Country* (New York, 1948), 271.
27 *Ibid.*, 273.
28 *The Mansion* (New York, 1959), 407.
29 *Ibid.*, 435-36.

CHAPTER VI

1 Marcus Dods (trans.), St. Augustine's *The City of God*, xiv. 13 (Modern Library Edition; New York, 1950), 460.
2 *Free Fall* (New York, 1959), 6.
3 *Ibid.*, 192.
4 *Ibid.*, 248.
5 *Ibid.*, 7.
6 Translated by Richard Lattimore, in Lattimore and David Grene (eds.), *The Complete Greek Tragedies* (4 vols.; Chicago, 1959), I, 169.
7 *The Man Who Died* (New York, 1959), 207.